TREASURES OF
TWO NATIONS

TREASURES OF TWO NATIONS

THAI ROYAL GIFTS
TO THE UNITED STATES OF AMERICA

LISA McQUAIL

ASIAN CULTURAL HISTORY PROGRAM

SMITHSONIAN INSTITUTION

1997

FRONT COVER:

CLOCKWISE FROM TOP RIGHT:

PHOTOGRAPH OF
H.M. KING CHULALONGKORN, RAMA V, on his
Second Coronation Day, 1873
Gift of King Chulalongkorn, 1876
Siam Exhibit, U.S. Centennial Exposition
NAA Neg. No. 041031.00

MODEL OF ROYAL BARGE SAMAT CHAI CLASS
เรือศรีสมรรถชัย
Rua Sri Samat Chai
Gift of King Chulalongkorn, 1876
Siam Exhibit, U.S. Centennial Exposition
USNM # 160278
168 cm length × 13 cm width

DETAIL OF PROW of the same Royal Barge model

PAINTING OF THE MOON GOD
"ดวงพระอาทิตย์"
Dwang Phra chan
Paint on canvas, mounted on tin
Gift of King Chulalongkorn, 1876
Siam exhibit, Centennial Exposition
USNM # 27209 (T-1378C)
24 cm diameter

ENDPAPERS:

Modified motif from
embroidered pillow
See: Fig. 97

Logo on title page and back cover
Blind embossing (hardcover edition only):
THUNDER GOD
Modified version of a shadow puppet.
See: Fig. 167.

BACK COVER:

TOP TO BOTTOM:

BASIN FOR WASHING THE FACE
"อ่างล้างหน้า"
Ang lang na
Part of a Toilette Set
Gift of King Chulalongkorn
Siam Exhibit, Centennial Exposition
Nielloware (silver, silver alloy, and gold)
USNM # 27148
18 cm height × 28.5 cm diameter

MONK'S ALMS BOWL, LID WITH EMBLEM OF
STATE, AND STAND
"บาท"(บาตร)
Bat
Gift of King Chulalongkorn, 1876
Siam Exhibit, Centennial Exposition
Wood, lacquer, mother-of-pearl
USNM #s 27266
30 cm total height

MASK OF VERMILLION DEMON SATASUN
Lord of Atsadong, friend of Thotsakan
"หน้าสะตสูร"
Na Satasun
Longka Army
Paper-mâché, paint, mirrors, and glass
Gift of King Chulalongkorn, 1876
Centennial Exposition, Siam Exhibit
USNM # 27385 (54235)
43 cm height × 26 cm width × 28 cm depth

FRONTISPIECE:

"WATER POT" ▶
"กาน้ำ"
Ka nam
Nielloware (silver, silver alloy, gold)
Gift of King Mongkut, 1856
Harris Treaty Gifts
USNM # 65
18 cm height × 11 cm diameter

Designed, typeset, printed, and bound by Oddi Printing, Iceland

Studio Photography by Diane L. Nordeck

© 1997 Smithsonian Institution

Library of Congress Cataloging-in-Publication Data (suggested)

McQuail, Lisa, 1960- [=McQuail, Belle Elizabeth ("Lisa"), 1960-]
Treasures of two nations: Thai royal gifts to the United States of America/ Lisa McQuail

p. cm.
Includes bibliographical references.
1. National Museum of Natural History (U.S.)-Ethnological collection-Catalogs. 2. Ethnological museums and collections-Catalogs. 3. Diplomatic gifts. 4. Material culture-Thailand-Catalogs. 5. Thailand-Foreign relations-United States. 6. United States-Foreign relations-Thailand.

I. National Museum of Natural History (U.S.). Asian Cultural History Program.

This book is produced and distributed by:
Asian Cultural History Program
Department of Anthropology
National Museum of Natural History
Smithsonian Institution
Washington DC 20560 USA

ISBN: 1-891739-01-8 (hardcover)
ISBN: 1-891739-02-6 (softcover)

FIG 1

5

MESSAGE FROM H.E. AMBASSADOR NITYA PIBULSONGGRAM

PREFACE AND ACKNOWLEDGEMENTS
by Paul Michael Taylor

Royal Thai Embassy
1024 Wisconsin Avenue, N.W., Suite 401
Washington, D.C. 20007
http://www.thaiembdc.org
e-mail : thai.wsn@thaiembdc.org
Tel. (202) 944-3600
Fax. (202) 944-3611

5 December 1996

December 5 is the date of the Birth of His Majesty King Bhumibol Adulyadej of Thailand. The Thai nation and people celebrate this date as their National Day.

Fifty years ago His Majesty the King, the ninth monarch of the Chakri Dynasty, ascended to the Throne.

We commemorate this auspicious day in this auspicious year with the publication of this book: Treasures of Two Nations: Thai Royal Gifts to the United States of America.

Thailand and the United States have been exchanging diplomatic gifts since our two nations signed the Treaty of Amity and Commerce in 1833 during the rule of King Nang Klao and President Andrew Jackson. That first treaty between Siam and The United States established a relationship of friendship, openness, and mutual support that has continued to renew itself with each succeeding generation.

The gifts that were exchanged between the two countries at the times of treaty signings under King Mongkut and President Franklin Pierce, and subsequently under King Chulalongkorn and President James Garfield are preserved and exhibited at the Smithsonian Institution in Washington, D.C. and the Grand Palace in Bangkok.

Since 1992 the Thai Government and in particular the Royal Thai Embassy in Washington, D.C. have been supporting The Heritage of Thailand project, a project of the Smithsonian Institution's National Museum of Natural History under its Anthropology Department's Asian Cultural History Program. The project has funded the conservation and documentation of this great collection of over 2,000 pieces.

During this, the Golden Jubilee of His Majesty King Bhumibol Adulyadej's accession to the throne, the Government and people of Thailand have given funding through the Heritage of Thailand for continued conservation and documentation of the Royal Gifts including the publication of this book.

The Heritage of Thailand project and the publication of this book are examples of the kind of mutually beneficial inter-governmental and scholarly links between our two nations that our great monarchs and presidents of the past envisioned for us. May these exquisite expressions of friendship echo in the hearts of our two peoples in all the years ahead.

Nitya Pibulsonggram
Ambassador

PREFACE AND ACKNOWLEDGEMENTS
by Paul Michael Taylor

By happy coincidence, two important anniversaries were celebrated in the year 1996; this book's year-long compilation began in celebration of both. Thailand and friends of Thailand everywhere celebrated the Fiftieth Anniversary of the Accession to the Throne of His Majesty, King Bhumibol Adulyadej, Rama IX. In America, the Smithsonian Institution, repository of America's precious Royal Gifts from the Kings of Thailand's Chakri Dynasty, was also celebrating its 150th anniversary.

The Thai Royal Gifts so admirably researched and illustrated in this volume are deeply symbolic of the long and evolving friendship between Thailand (formerly called Siam) and the United States of America. This study documents for the first time a group of artifacts whose meaning and significance have, until now, been inadequately understood by scholars, and sometimes even misunderstood by the recipients of the gifts themselves–the presidents and people of the United States. Yet for both Thais and Americans these gifts truly are historic, artistic, and scientific treasures, through which the Kings of Thailand represented their nation, and its alliances with America through time. Nearly all sets of gifts, from the courtly gold nielloware, silks, musical instruments and weapons to the everyday basketry, tools, agricultural samples and fish traps, were accompanied by a Royal Letter listing the contents of the gift (in Thai and English), and explaining its significance. This catalog introduces those Royal Letters and their lists, for the first time, into the interpretation of the gifts. This book will interest art-, social-, and diplomatic-historians; anthropologists, linguists, and ethnomusicologists; students of Thai theater and culture; and all those who will appreciate the aesthetic quality of the gift objects or the very good stories those objects were meant to tell.

The catalog offered here is the product of Lisa McQuail's research over an eight-year period. That research was sponsored in part by the Smithsonian's "Heritage of Thailand" project, established in 1982 for "conservation, restoration, and research of the Thai collections" within the Asian Cultural History Program. Her task was challenging, for the original documentation for this magnificent collection, as for so many others, had been scattered among many institutions and archives. Most of all, the collections themselves needed careful conservation and a climate-controlled, state-of-the-art environment for their long-term preservation. Since 1982, a very major conservation effort has been completed, and all the Thai collections that are not on display have been moved to an up-to-date new Smithsonian facility for preservation and research.

Just as the objects' proper physical care required conservation and re-housing on a large scale, the proper historic documentation of each individual object required interpreting this collection of Royal Gifts in its entirety. Matching the objects with museum registrarial records and archival documents has been a rewarding job of detective-work, since museum registration in the past did not always meet today's standards. Even the very first list of Smithsonian ethnology accessions in our oldest ledger-book accidentally mixed objects from Commodore Perry's 1854 Japan Expedition with the gifts sent by H.M. King Mongkut in 1856! Over the years, some labels fell off, objects got re-named, and early collections were even re-numbered in ill-conceived attempts to organize them, apparently without access to the original gift lists. Thankfully a good paper trail, in the form of internal Smith-

Seal of the 50th Anniversary of the Accession to the Throne of Thailand of His Majesty, King Bhumibol Adulyadej.

150th Anniversary Seal, Smithsonian Institution

sonian documents, correspondence in the U.S. National Archives, and some published exhibit records (e.g., the 1876 Siam Exhibit), has now been examined and reconstructed, giving new life and historic depth to a magnificent collection.

This catalog should therefore serve as a thoughtful, illustrated introduction to this collection and its historic significance, and hopefully also as a stimulus for many other, more specialized studies of these treasures of two nations.

This book, truly a collaborative project, was made possible by a generous donation from the Royal Thai Government to the Smithsonian's "Heritage of Thailand" fund. The donation was made in 1996, in commemoration of the fiftieth anniversary of the accession to the throne of His Majesty, King Bhumibol Adulyadej, Rama IX. The Smithsonian gratefully acknowledges the help of the Royal Thai Embassy in Washington, especially H.E. Ambassador Nitya Pibulsonggram, for sharing the initial vision for this book, and for providing many helpful suggestions. His letter of December 5, 1996, introduces this book. Other invaluable help was provided by Embassy staff, especially Minister (and Deputy Chief of Mission) Akrasid Amatayakul and Minister Counsellor Malinda Manoonchai. We owe a very special debt of thanks to Mom Rajawongse Putrie Viravaidya, General Secretary of the Privy Council at the Grand Palace in Bangkok, who took so much time from her busy schedule to advise the Smithsonian throughout our work on the Thai collections, and specifically on the contents of this book.

The "Heritage of Thailand" project, under whose auspices this book is produced, was initiated in conjunction with an exhibition of Thai Royal Gifts at the Smithsonian's National Museum of Natural History in 1982, in celebration of the Chakri Dynasty bicentennial. The project received much support at its founding from H.E. Ambassador Prok Amaranand, and further help later from his successors including H.E. Ambassador M.L. Birabhongse Kasemsri and H.E. Ambassador Manaspas Xuto; also from former Counsellor Wilaiwan Chompoopet and former Second Secretary Pitchya Sookmark. Thai Airways International, Ltd., has generously provided air transportation for this project; we especially thank Mr. Ton Loharjun of Thai Airways's Washington office. IBM Corporation has also provided essential computer support through the Asian Cultural History Program's "Virtual Museum" project. Generous support has also been provided by Texaco and by Caltex Petroleum Corporation.

Our Heritage of Thailand project has also been helped, within Thailand, by the hospitality of Mr. Mechai Viravaidya, and by M.R. Disnadda Diskul and the staff of the Mae Fah Luang Foundation, particularly Ms. Buranee Buranasiri, Dr. Charles B. Mehl, and Mr. Nakorn Pongnoi; by Dr. Sasithara Pichaichannarong of the National Culture Commission; by Dr. Smitthi Siribhadra of Silpakorn University; and by Mr. Bangkok Chowkwanyun and Nyle Spoelstra of The Siam Society.

Many Smithsonian staff and associates contributed to this book. For all their help, we thank the Director of the National Museum of Natural History, Robert W. Fri, and former Director Donald J. Ortner; Anthropology Department Chair Dennis J. Stanford, and Deputy Chair Carolyn L. Rose; Collection Management staff Deborah Hull-Walski, Johanna Humphrey, Natalie Firnhaber, Felicia Pickering, Susan Crawford, and Alice Thomson; Anthropology librarians Margaret Dittemore and Mayda Riopedre, and former librarian Mary Kay Davies. We are especially grateful to Diane Nordeck for the studio photography of Royal Gifts in our collections, made possible through the help of Harold "Doc" Dougherty and Lori H. Aceto, and with additional photographic help from Eric Long and Carl Hansen. We also acknowledge the important assistance of Francine Berkowitz and Brian W.J. Le May at the Office of International Relations; Alan Ullberg at the Office of General Counsel; Lisa Keenan and Sherylle Mills at the Office of Contracting; and

Marcia Bakry, T.C. Benson, Paula Fleming, Heidi Gjerset, Damon C. Hill, Randall Kremer, Kurt Luginbyhl, Johnna Miller, Vichai Malikul, Bryan Sieling, Joyce Sommers, Jonathan Spangler, Marjory Stoller, Robert Sullivan, and Randy S. Tims of the National Museum of Natural History. Like most museums, our work depends on dedicated volunteers, among whom Carl Barrow, Georgia Reilly, Winifred Weislogel, Napa Promjak, and Wiranrong Boonuch deserve special mention for their invaluable help with this project.

Catherine Rhodes served as editorial project coordinator for the Asian Cultural History Program; Ellyn Allison copy-edited the manuscript. Professor H. Leedom Lefferts of Drew University, who is also a Research Associate within the Smithsonian's Asian Cultural History Program, made substantial contributions to the coordination and editing of this book. Among the many other scholars who helped with the Heritage of Thailand project over the years are: Sylvia Fraser-Lu, Mattiebelle Gittinger, Milton Gustafson, Thomas Kirsch, Lisa Lyons, Forrest McGill, William R. Tuchrello, and David K. Wyatt; also the Abbott and monks of Wat Thummapratiep (Alexandria, Virginia), including Phra Maha Sutham Kannathip, Phra Maha Jamnong Phrasongsook, Phra Maha Sanit Poonsawat, and Phra Sompak Vachiro, Phra Khru Sujin Piangtiang, and Phra Wichai Poonyawichayo.

For the book's design and production, we thank many people at Oddi Printing Corporation, especially Árni Sigurðsson (president), Björn S. Víðisson (project manager), Jón Ellert Sverrisson (production manager), Halldór Þorsteinsson (designer), Eyjólfur Jónsson (typesetting manager), Rúnar Vilhjálmsson (computer layout), Sigrún Karlsdóttir (copy editor), Díana Lanthom Huiphimai (Thai typesetting), Kesara Anamthawat-Jónsson (Thai editing), Þórdís Einarsdóttir (computer technician), Eyjólfur Eyjólfsson (scanning and color balancing), and Björn Fróðason (chief computer technician).

After listing such distinguished supporters of this project, and reviewers of or contributors to this work, the author and all Smithsonian staff involved would hasten to add that this book's defects and shortcomings are, like the book's final form and content, entirely our responsibility.

Paul Michael Taylor
Director, Asian Cultural History Program
National Museum of Natural History
Smithsonian Institution
December 5, 1997

TECHNICAL NOTES

The Romanization of Thai Words

Personal names of Thai Royalty follow English spellings used by the Royal Secretariat. Other romanizations of Thai words and proper names generally follow the Royal Institute's "General System of Phonetic Transcription of Thai Characters into Roman" (see Varnvaidya 1941). Exceptions have been made for the proper names of persons who have chosen, or whose families have chosen, an alternative romanization of their own names (for example, H.R.H. Prince Wan Waitayakorn).

◄◄ Detail of Interior, Siam Pavilion, Louisiana Purchase Exposition, 1904. Library of Congress, Prints and Photographs, Frances Benjamin Johnston Collection.

Photo Captions and Catalog Records

Many of the Royal Gifts in Smithsonian collections were accompanied by descriptions in both Thai and English, in lists of gifts that were included in Royal Letters to the U.S. Presidents (see, Figures 28A and 28B). Since these inventories were prepared as long ago as 1856, many have archaic spellings and word choices. When available, those names from the original Thai and English gift lists are included here within quotation marks. Following that, when necessary for clarification, current Thai and English equivalents are also presented.

The conventions used for catalog numbers and transliterations in the photo captions are used throughout the text. When referring to the King, or to the belongings and actions of a Thai King, Thais use a special court language called *rajasap* These words are sometimes capitalized in English here (for example, "King," "Royal Letter," and "Royal Barge") in order to convey the extreme respect that Thais give them through the use of court language.

Photo captions give the following information: (1) name in English, followed by (2) name in Thai with (3) romanization of the Thai term (each may optionally have, within quotes, the archaic English or Thai terms, or the archaic romanization of the term, as used in original Gift Lists); (4) the donor and date of gift, sometimes with additional information about the associated treaty, exhibition, or context of the gift; (5) the object's catalog number; and (6) measurements of the gift object. The catalog number is preceded by an abbreviation denoting the Smithsonian museum or "curatorial unit" in which the object is catalogued, as follows:

USNM – (formerly) United States National Museum, now The National Museum of Natural History, Smithsonian Institution. (All "USNM" objects included here are from the Ethnology Division, Department of Anthropology.)

NAA – National Anthropological Archives (Department of Anthropology, National Museum of Natural History)

RB – Dibner Rare Book Library, Smithsonian Institution

Other cited records and information come from the U.S. National Archives, the U.S. Library of Congress, or other institutions, each credited where appropriate in the text.

FIG 2

FLAG OF SIAM
"ธงสยามรัฐ"
Hand-painted cotton, appliquéd
Gift of King Chulalongkorn, 1881
Harris Treaty Revisions Gifts
USNM # 168493
180.3 cm length × 270.45 cm width

14

THAI ROYAL GIFTS
TO THE UNITED STATES OF AMERICA:
A HISTORICAL PERSPECTIVE

1. THE SMITHSONIAN'S COLLECTION OF THAI ROYAL GIFTS

The Smithsonian Institution's collection of Thai Royal Gifts to the Presidents and people of the United States are an important part of the diplomatic history of both nations. Siam (now the Kingdom of Thailand)[1] was the first Asian nation to sign a treaty with the United States. This long-lasting friendship began informally in the 1820s with the first of many American merchants and missionaries in Thailand. The relationship was more formally established under King Nang Klao, Rama III, with the first treaty between the United States and Thailand, the "Treaty of Amity and Commerce" of 1833. The treaty was negotiated for the U.S. by Envoy Edmund Roberts, who had been sent to Bangkok by President Andrew Jackson. From the first formal exchange of gifts accompanying that treaty in 1833 to this day, the Thai monarchs have continued to give the American presidents and people gifts that promote understanding and friendship between these two nations.[3] Thailand's present monarchs, His Majesty King Bhumibol Adulyadej and Her Majesty Queen Sirikit, in addition to giving gifts of state to the presidents, have taken an interest in many American universities and other institutions including the Smithsonian.

The Smithsonian's collections of nineteenth-century Thai material is one of the finest and best documented in the world. This collection is unusual because it includes a great number of common objects from everyday life in nineteenth- and twentieth-century Thailand, as well as the courtly items one would expect in Royal Gifts. The collection is certainly an important scholarly resource and the objects themselves posess great dignity and beauty, whether made from gold or silk in the court or made of rattan or cotton in a remote village. More importantly, these objects are the gifts of Thai Kings representing all of their people in reaching out to the United States since the 1830s–when America was a new but powerful nation that would later prove to be Thailand's valued ally. The exchange of gifts sealed a friendship between two very different nations, and are symbols of a friendship that endures to this day.

The two countries have exchanged many gifts over the years. Many of the gifts sent by America to Thailand are on display at the Grand Palace in Bangkok.[4] Fifteen major sets of gifts were formally exchanged in 1833, 1856, 1861, 1876, 1881, 1884, 1893, 1904, 1927, 1960, 1966, 1967, 1982, and 1995, and 1996. King Nang Klao, Rama III, initiated the first round of formal diplomatic gift exchange between Thailand and America in 1833 on the occasion of the first treaty between the two countries, known as the Roberts Treaty. Because of a cultural misunderstanding, and because of the perishable nature of that royal gift (a collection of rare rainforest products), it was not retained by the US government. Happily, history has left us with a list of those items (see "Gifts of Mutual Respect," below).[5] The Smithsonian's collection begins with the next set of gifts which King Mongkut and his

◄◄ The white elephant on a red field was a powerful symbol for the Asian nation of Siam.

Asian elephants have served royalty in Persia, India and Southeast Asia for millennia in warfare, as transportation, and as the workforce in harvesting of the riches of the rain forest. White elephants are actually gray with pink patches, especially on the ears and around the eyes.[2] These markings are thought to be auspicious, and white elephants were keenly sought by Asian courts and pampered as symbols of luck and prosperity. This design was replaced by the current red, white, and blue flag during the 1920s by King Vajiravudh (Rama VI).

---

[1] In 1939 the English name "Siam" was changed to "Thailand." Because the material presented here spans both periods, for the sake of simplicity "Thailand" and "Thai" will be used throughout.
[2] For a richly illustrated description of the importance of the elephant in Asian history, see Delort 1992.
[3] See Appendix: List of Chakri Dynasty Kings
[4] Krairiksh 1985 volume 4, on King Mongkut, Rama IV, shows some of the gifts from Queen Victoria on display at the Grand Palace. King Mongkut proudly showed these gifts as well as the gold "Eagle and Elephant" sword given to Rama III by President Andrew Jackson, to Townsend Harris and other Western visitors (Wood 1859, p. 206; Cosenza 1930). Phra Pinklao also had gifts from Western nations on display at the Front Palace, Wang Na, as witnessed by that same group (Wood 1859, p. 209).
[5] An account of the 1833 United States mission to Southeast Asia, including some of Edmund Roberts' journal entries, is published in the journal of the USS Peacock's surgeon, Dr. Benjah Ticknor, in Hodges 1991.

brother, the "Second King" Phra Pinklao gave in 1856 to commemorate the signing of the Harris Treaty. In 1861 King Mongkut, Rama IV sent a Royal Letter and a further set of Royal Gifts to President James Buchanan. Those gifts are now kept in the U.S. National Archives.[6] The Harris Treaty of 1856 was revised in 1882, and gifts were exchanged at that time also. King Chulalongkorn specified that these ethnological gifts from rural Thailand and the accompanying flag and "Gifts of Respect" should be deposited directly to the Smithsonian's collections. In addition, former President Grant (who stopped by to visit King Chulalongkorn in Bangkok on his post-presidential World Tour) and other American citizens donated their own personal Thai Royal Gifts to the Smithsonian.[7]

Outside of the formal diplomatic gift exchange system, usually carried on between heads of state during or after treaty negotiations or state visits, Thailand also gave gifts to the United States on other occasions. The Thais participated in several world expositions held in the United States in the late nineteenth and early twentieth centuries. The contents of these exhibits were given in whole or in part to the United States as direct Royal Gifts by Royal Decree, and are now in the Smithsonian's collections. These gifts include the entire contents of the Siam Exhibit at the 1876 Centennial Exposition, held in Philadelphia (over 900 objects), small parts of the Siam Exhibit from the New Orleans Exposition of 1884 and the World's Columbia Exposition of 1893, and part of the Siam Exhibit displayed in the Agricultural Hall at the 1904 Louisiana Purchase Exposition, held in St. Louis (over 300 objects).

Thailand also gave gifts to mark important occasions for both nations, such as the 25th Anniversary of King Chulalongkorn, Rama V's Accession to the Throne (1893), and the Centennial of the birth of James Smithson, founder of the Smithsonian Institution (1967).

The history and meaning of Thai Royal Gifts and the circumstances of Thai-American gift exchange that brought Thai Royal Gifts to the Smithsonian Institution are the subject of this volume.

2. THAILAND AND ASIAN GIFT EXCHANGE

In the history of Asia, stories of war and conflict abound. Against this background, the history of Thai diplomacy is a story of the wisdom of Thai kings and the epic journeys of their diplomats who bore splendid gifts and beautiful, formal letters that were works of art in themselves. It is also a story of the Thai court's tendency to welcome and tolerate foreign visitors, foreign ideas, and foreign trade. While it is possible to classify levels of gifts and to describe the waxing and waning of Asian alliances in a clear hierarchy of powers that developed over time, what is most important is that alliances and friendships were sought and kept through Thailand's gestures of gift-giving and through Thailand's gesture of welcoming foreigners into Thai society.[8]

Thailand's role in regional Southeast Asian politics and economy has always been an important one. Many Thai products and natural resources were highly sought after by other nations. Thailand's forests yielded rare and beautiful hardwoods prized for their suitability in furniture and interiors, fragrant woods used in insence and perfumes, and resins valued as both adhesives and medicines. In addition, Thailand's fishing and rice production were often plentiful enough to send the surplus abroad in trade.

Thailand and other Asian nations exchanged embassies and gifts, usually in three-year cycles, which reaffirmed alliances between nations and allowed for the development of further trade. The city-kingdom of Ayutthaya, the capital of the

[6] The letter, sword, photograph of King Mongkut and one of his children, and "cigarette case" are illustrated in Viola 1984, p. 96-97.

[7] The Smithsonian's Thai materials include donations of personal collections from later American missionaries to Thailand, such as those of Dr. George Bradley McFarland and Dr. Samuel House. These American missionary doctors of the early twentieth century carried on the work of an earlier generation of American missionaries to Thailand, active from the 1840s to the 1880s, who were teachers and advisors in the court as well as missionaries. Two longtime residents of Bangkok, missionary Dr. Stephen J. Matoon and missionary, teacher, advisor and engineer Rev. John Hasset Chandler, acted as the first two United States consuls.

[8] See Wilson 1970 in which the political hierarchy of Asian nations in the nineteenth century is discussed.

Thais from 1378-1767, was highly cosmopolitan as a result of centuries Asian diplomacy and economic relations.

Records of gifts and tribute received by Thailand during the Ayutthaya period document exchanges of gifts that were both economically valuable and symbolic.[9] Thus when Europeans arrived in Thailand in the early 16th century, they were easily incorporated into the Asian and Thai gift exchange systems.

3. THE MEANING OF THAI ROYAL GIFTS

Gifts exchanged by Western delegations and the Thais often filled true needs carefully researched by both the Thai court and the Western missions.[10] There are three basic types of Royal Gifts to foreign delegations: first, the "Official Welcome" consisting of gifts of lodging, enourmous amounts of beautifully arrayed provisions, and personal gifts to emissaries; second, the "Gift of Mutual Respect" *Khru'ang Ratchabannakan*, a presentation of Thai forest products and agricultural products indicating respect to the receiving nation and a simple overture to trade in these items; and third, the *Phraratchathan*–gift of a set of insignia of rank to equal or subordinate nations.[11] Insignia of rank include all of the items that the foreign head-of-state would need to survive in the Thai court including clothing, weapons, religious items, and modes of transportation. These gifts of insignia were lavish and often could fill the entire hold of a European ship. Most of the time the Thai kings chose to begin foreign relations with an official welcome and an initial "Gift of Mutual Respect," and gave the insignia of rank gifts as a distinctly separate presentation. Since each Thai Royal Gift was accompanied by a Royal Letter which included lists of gifts, it is clear that the two types of gifts were intended as separate presentations.[12] It seems that in the European records of Thai gifts, often the two types of gifts were intermingled.

GIFTS OF WELCOME

Overtures to friendship and gestures of hospitality were just as important to the Thai court and Western visitors as overtures to trade. Even when the Thais were not in the position to negotiate a treaty, delegations were welcomed to the court. Western missions to the Thai court were welcomed with hospitality and the visits occasioned many rounds of gift exchange between the court and the emmissaries in addition to the more formal exchanges of gifts between the two sovereign nations. Unfortunately, pure hospitality was often misinterpreted by foreign emissaries, who were disappointed by what they seemed to perceive as "mixed signals" if treaty negotiations that followed their welcome went poorly. Examples of the Thai tradition of *ton rap kæk* "welcoming of guests" can be seen in every account of foreign missions to the Ayutthaya and Bangkok courts. On "crossing the bar" at the mouth of the Chao Phraya River, Sir John Bowring's 1856 British mission was met at the *entrepôt* of Paknam with a delegation delivering a letter of welcome and instructions from King Mongkut.

"They had a quantity of fruit, sent by the King–mangoes, oranges, lichis, ananas [pineapples], plaintains, and several specimens unknown to me–all in richly ornamented silver salvers, with a variety of sweetmeats, covered with banana leaves. Another boat followed, with a large display of cocoa-nuts, sugar canes, one hundred fowls, ducks, pigs, eggs, rice, paddy, etc., for the use of our crews."[13]

[9] Wilson 1970, Chandler 1982, and Wyatt 1975 offer historical interpretations of the Asian gift exchange network.

[10] For background on pre-nineteenth century trade and negotiations in Southeast Asia, see Reid 1988, 1993; Tarling 1992. Regarding Thailand's relations with other Asian polities, see Wilson 1970, Wyatt 1975, 1984. Regarding gifts as objects, see articles in Thatcher and Taylor 1995.

[11] Wilson 1970, Chandler 1982, and Wyatt 1975, were used as the basis for this examination of the Asian gift exchange network, as were anthropological treatises on gift exhchange such as Marcel Mauss' *The Gift* (1967). The Yale-Smithsonian Seminar "The Gift as Material Culture" held April 28-30, 1991 was also a source of inspiration, particularly papers given by Taylor (p. 3-14), Jessup (pp. 45-47) and Fern (pp. 48-49) (Thatcher and Taylor 1991). John Chandler's account of King Mongkut's decision to give President Franklin Pierce a gift of the same composition as that given to Thai high-ranking princes and officials (U.S. National Archives, R.G 59 Consular Dispatches, 1856) was the piece of information that established, for this author, the meaning of the Thai gifts of state in the context of the traditional Thai Royal Gift. The author then examined the category of items given in the Thai traditional Royal Gift as shown by Wilson and Wyatt, and compared them with the Siam exhibits at Western expositions, and observed that they always included a traditional Thai Royal Gift befitting the rank of the head of state of the hosting nation. This study was followed by an examination of the changing nature of the Thai Royal Gift into the twentieth century. The author presented this material in a slide lecture given at the Smithsonian Institution on October 4th, 1991, at the "Seminar in Honor of the Centennial of the Birth of Prince Wan Waitayakorn". Lists of "Gifts of Mutual Respect" were examined, and a clear pattern emerged, as many of these groupings had a core of products in common. Considering the formal way in which these items were usually presented and upon researching the traditional uses of each item, it became clear that these groups of useful forest animal and agricultural products were given as both a sign of respect and an overture to trade. The author's research was supported by the Smithsonian's "Heritage of Thailand" project, gratefully acknowledged here.

[12] US National Archives, Record Group 59, Diplomatic Records. Smithsonian Institution, Accession Records, Department of Anthropology, Siam records, 1882.

[13] Bowring 1857, Vol I, p. 251

William Maxwell Wood, Ship's Surgeon of the *USS San Jacinto*, American envoy Townsend Harris's ship, noted that while they were at anchor at Paknam, a boat arrived at their side. "It proved to be a boat of presents from the king. Twelve hundred pounds of sugar, four chests of fine tea, piles of fruit, and hundreds of cocoanuts and fowls, with four pigs. . ."[14] Crawfurd, Bowring, and Harris all remarked that the court insisted on providing them with money to cover their other expenses while in Bangkok, and each mission was given a house which was continually resupplied with provisions by various members of the court each day. Ship's Surgeon Wood took careful note of this hospitality: "All the cooks, servants, and the provisions of this establishment, together with three boats, with from twenty to thirty rowers, or rather paddlers, in each, were furnished by the king. And the expense of our reception and entertainment must have more than equaled the value of our presents to the king."[15]

The kings also gave many personal gifts to the envoys. King Mongkut, for instance, gave Bowring two young elephants, but since there was not adequate room in the ship, Bowring had to leave them behind.[16] The kings often granted informal interviews to the envoys in addition to the formal audiences required for the presentation of letters and gifts of heads of state.

King Mongut invited both Bowring and Harris to his private apartments at the Grand Palace for informal talks and to view *Khon* theater performances. On one of these occasions, Townsend Harris gave King Mongkut the *Nautical Almanac* for 1856, 1857, and 1858, and King Mongkut ". . .gave me a silver gilt segar (sic) case filled with segars (sic)."[17] Phra Pin Klao, King Mongkut's brother and the "Second King" gave Sir John Bowring gifts during a private tea at this very Western-style palace. "He gave me a Laos wind instrument of bamboo (very sweet), which he said had been presented to him by the Prince of Laos; also a Laos sword, a collection of coins, and other marks of kindness. He read me the letter he had written for the Queen [Queen Victoria], of which I recommended him to send also a Siamese version. Tea, etc. was poured out for us by the King himself, with the grace of perfect good breeding."[18]

Finally, what is reflected in these private, informal audiences is the gift of friendship, time, and personal attention given by each of the kings and of the high-ranking members of the Thai court to the foreign emissaries.

GIFTS SHOWING MUTUAL RESPECT:

Khru'ang Ratchabannakan

Thailand received tribute from many outlying regions and kingdoms of Southeast Asia. Exchanges of "tribute" and Thai "Gifts of Mutual Respect" probably have their origins in very ancient giftgiving customs in Asia. These sets of gifts are the ones that looked most strange to Western eyes, for they were composed of collections of elephant tusks, incense, exotic woods, foodgoods, medicines, spices, perfumes and resins from Thailand's forests and agricultural fields. The court of Thailand received much of this forest bounty as tribute from leaders in the outlying provinces, and as such they are symbolic of the Thai court's rule over a vast and varied territory. When these forest riches were given as gifts to other Asian Heads-of-State, the Thai called these gifts *Khru'ang Ratchabannakan*. These gifts should be regarded from the perspective of symbol and ritual and as a simple overture to trade, for in all practicality even the most lavish of Asian gifts of respect consisted of only a small percentage of the production of luxury, medicinal, and foodgoods of a nation.

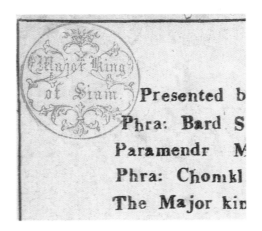

[14] Wood 1859, p. 159.

[15] Wood 1859, p. 167. In general, Wood's account of the American mission of 1856 is more complete than Harris', and Wood certainly showed an appreciation for Thai culture and diplomacy that Harris seemed to lack entirely.

[16] Thai kings often wished to include elephants in sets of gifts to Western heads of state, however, more often than not, the elephants were left behind due to lack of room in ships holds. This was the case with King Narai's 1686 gift of elephants to Louis XIV (Smithies 1990), with King Mongkut's 1855 gift of elephants to Sir John Bowring. King Mongkut's proposed gift of elephants to the United States was rejected on the grounds that America's climate was unsuitable. (US National Archives, RG 59, Ceremonial Letters.)

[17] Cosenza 1930, p. 162. Harris, aware of the US government's restrictions on gifts, professed "I shall smoke those and send the case to the Secretary of State".

[18] Bowring 1857, Vol II, p. 331

[19] See Chandler 1982.

[20] Smith 1977 p. 148-151. Identifications and uses are from Burkhill 1966.

[21] The Thai court was uncomfortable with the prospect of dealing with the mercantile Dutch East India Company alone, and asked company officials to establish a direct link between the Thai king and the Dutch Royal Family (Smith 1977).

Southeast Asian gift-giving reflected the region's gradations of status and myriads of ever-shifting alliances, in which nations were constantly emerging in new positions in the hierarchy of diplomacy, gift-exchange, and economic relations.[19] The "Gift of Mutual Respect" was often a good choice for the Thai Kings to send to powerful nations, since these collections of rare products indicated respect as well as an overture to trade in those very same products of forest and field.

According to Smith,[20] after initial contact between the Thai court and the Dutch royal family (the House of Orange)[21] the following list of products (arranged here for simplicity by type of product) which are also commonly included in "Gifts of Respect" eventually formed the major items of Dutch trade in Ayutthaya:

Animal Products

Birds' nests [edible bird's nests of Hume's swiftlet (*Collocalia innominata*) prized as an ingredient to a tonic soup]

Bird plumes

Buffalo hides [(*Bos bubalus*) exported to Japan]

Buffalo horn [(*Bos bubalus*) used for carving into boxes and for kris handles, also used medicinally]

Cow hides [exported to Japan]

Deer hides [(both *Cervidae* and *Tragulidae*) exported to Japan]

Elephant tusks [carved for jewelry, furniture inlay, and sculpture]

Gumlac [(*Laccifer lacca [Coccidae]*) Lacquer, shellac, and red dye that comes from *L. Lacca*, a swarming insect.]

Ray skins [used as buffing "sand paper" in woodworking, used by Japanese on sword hilts]

Rhinoceros horns [prized for medicinal use, particularly to promote male potency, by Chinese]

Silk

Beeswax

Plant Products

Benzoin [(*Styrax benzoides* or *S. Tonkinense*) used by Asians for skin complaints and reumatic conditions]

Betel nut [(*Piper betle*) chewed with a mixture of other ingredients which together form a mild narcotic]

Black Lac [(*Rhus [Anacardiaceae]*). Most probably *R. succedanea*, the more southerly species, which yields lacquer]

Cardamom [(*Elettaria cardamomum.*) Used by Chinese as medicine, by Europeans and Southeast Asians as a spice, and by Southeast Asians as part of the betel quid]

Coconut oil [(*Cocos*) fragrant oil used for protecting and caring for skin, in soaps and as a vehicle for medicines. Used magically in kris-making]

Eaglewood [(*Aquilaria*), "Calamba" or "Calambac" (aloes wood, also known as Eagle wood) is resin-filled wood from diseased *Aquilaria*, and is valued as incense]

Gittagum [Probably *getah*, Malay for sap or latex]

Indigo [(*Indigofera*) source of blue dye used throughout the world]

Ironwood [a wood prized for its hardness and resistance to insect damage. Used for firewood, poles and posts, support structures in buildings, etc.]

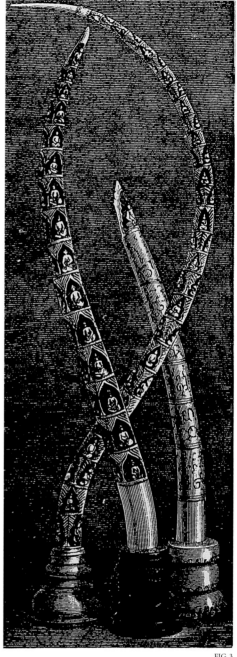

FIG 3

ENGRAVING OF CARVED ELEPHANT TUSKS
Gifts of King Chulalongkorn, Rama V
Siam Exhibit, Centennial Exposition
Frank Leslie's Illustrated Historical Register of the Centennial Exposition, 1876

Elephant tusks were an important part of a "Gift of Mutual Respect," and represented the control of the Thai court over a number of valuable White Elephants as well as the availability of highly trained Thai work elephants, war elephants, and their beautiful, carvable tusks, valuable to Thailand's trading partners.

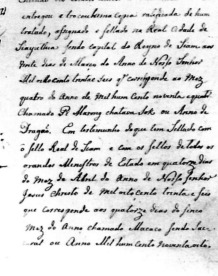

กกกลฑพระโฉนกพา

Paddy (unhusked rice) [(*Oryza sativa*) Cheaper than husked rice, paddy was threshed after purchase. The hulls were used for packing material and as fuel]

Pepper [(*Piper*) used as spice]

Radix China [(*Smilax China*) Used by Europeans for treating syphilis]

Raw sugar [probably palm sugar]

Rose-mallows [liquid storax]

Saffron [(*Crocus*) used as a colorful yellow spice]

Sandalwood [(*Santalum album*) a parasitic tree that yields a fragrant wood used for cosmetics, medicines, and incense]

Sapanwood [(*Caesalpinia sappan*) used for red and violet dye, but also used medicinally throughout Southeast Asia]

Precious Metals and Minerals

Copper

Gold

Lead

Spelter (pewter)

Tin (Cassiterite)

Such products had long been of vital importance in Asia for their value as medicines, ingredients for the production of fine arts, as drugs and medicines, and as spices. Despite the fact that they also became vitally important in European life, especially after intensive promotion as medicines, spices, and luxury materials by Dutch merchants, Westerners probably did not recognize these materials in their raw forms. This oversight, in addition to Westerners' lack of understanding of the tribute as an overture to trade, caused Westerners to be disdainful of these gifts.

For instance in 1833, US Envoy Edmund Roberts was disappointed with the gift of respect from the Thais, as he expressed in his journal.[22] "Yesterday and today a variety of presents was sent to the Envoy, from the Chao Phia Phra Klang (sic) [the Thai equivalent of foreign minister]. They consisted of elephant's teeth (sic) [tusks], sugar (*nam tan*), sugar-candy, pepper, cardammus [*Amomum krervanh*, or *Elettaria* sp.] (krawan) gambooge (sic) [*Garcinia hanburyi*] (*rong tong*), agila [*Aquilaria agallocha*] (*maykrisana*), sopan [sapanwood (*Caesalpinia sappan*) used for red and violet dye, but also used medicinally throughout Southeast Asia] wood (sic) [*Caesalpinia sappan*] *mayfang*), etc."[23] The significance of these items was apparently not recognized by the United States as these items were not retained, but in fact the Americans would have been pleased had they realized that the collection of things was a gift of respect, or *Khruang Ratchabannakan*. Roberts and the Americans did not seem to realize that although the Thais constructed what the Americans thought was a restrictive treaty, they sent a very respectful gift which was itself a strong overture to trade in the eyes of the Thai court.

[22] An account of the 1833 United States mission to Southeast Asia, including some of Roberts's journal entries, is published in the journal of the Peacock's surgeon, Dr. Benjah Ticknor, in Hodges 1991. In general, Ticknor's account is more detailed than Roberts's official report (Roberts, 1833, Diplomatic Records, RG 59, U. S. National Archives).

[23] Roberts, 1833, Diplomatic Records, RG 59, U. S. National Archives. Linnaean identifications from Burkhill 1966.

FIG 4

THAI ROYAL GIFTS OF INSIGNIA OF RANK
Phraratchathan

Thai Royal Gifts to heads of state were patterned after formal Thai Insignia of rank. These sets of insignia were given by the king to his Royal relatives, his queens and royal princes and princesses, to mark their status, and were given to members of the civil nobility when the king bestowed their ranks upon them. Sets of insignia were often acquired over time, for the king could add to an insignia set at will. The most important purpose of such sets of insignia was to ensure that each person in the court had the "uniform" or "costume" of clothing, insignia, weapons, and other utensils necessary to be a part of every court pagent and necessary for the daily life of a person of rank. European accounts of the activities of the Thai court recount many court processions, describing the entrances of the Thai princes and officials to an audience with the king. Harris noted this on during his 1865 audience with King Mongkut.

> "Arrived at the Hall of Justice, the nobles. . . [were] dressed in rich gowns interwoven with gold. Everyone had the insignia of his rank,–*viz.*, a gold betelnut box, gold teapot, swords, etc., near him."[24]

Since production of these items was highly regulated by the court, no one could posess them except through the king's largess. To some extent, in addition to a yearly stipend from the court, royal and noble princes could acquire monetary wealth through their land-holdings and through trade of certain items deemed proper by the king. This money was used to purchase virtually anything of interest and use–there are records showing that Thai royalty and nobility purchased everything from Indian cloth to steamship parts on the open market. However, poses-

SET OF NEILLOWARE ITEMS
Gift of King Chulalongkorn
Siam Exhibit, Centennial Exposition
Engraving from *Frank Leslie's Illustrated Historical Register of the Centennial Exposition, 1876*

---

[24] Cosenza 1930, p. 132.

sion of elaborate insignia of rank, the most important marks of status in Thai society, was highly controlled and funneled through the king at his discretion.

Gifts to heads of state had a further purpose: to dazzle the foreign head of state with the high quality, wonderful variety, and sheer number of the gifts. Enormous time and effort were required by the Thai court to assemble these gifts.[25] It is clear from accounts of the Thai mission to Versailles in 1686 that the lengthy compilation of Royal Letters and the sheer volume of the Thai Royal Gifts to Versailles, which filled two French vessels to capacity, had sorely taxed the patience of the French, especially Abbé de Choisy, the French co-adjutant ambassador assigned the task of preparing a list of King Narai's gifts in French for presentation with the Royal Letters. He declared of the list "It will be a book." His list is peppered with phrases that show his despair at his task, such as, after the entry for item 53, "eighty-four pieces of porcelain. . . with many other valuable Presents to Madam the Daughiness, which I am weary of relating."

FIG 5B

WATERPOT "กาน้ำ" *KA NAM*
Niello ware (silver, silver alloy, gold)
Gift of Phra Pin Klao, Uparat (Second King),
1856
Harris Treaty Gifts
USNM # 62
Height 20.5 cm × diameter 15 cm.

NEILLOWARE ITEMS
Gifts of King Chulalongkorn, 1876
Siam Exhibit, Centennial Exposition
USNM #s 57, 58, 59, 60, 61, 62

FIG 5

In his letter to Franklin Pierce dated May 9, 1856, King Mongkut notes that envoy Townsend Harris intended to leave only two days after the 1856 treaty was ratified,

". . .in which most narrow space in time we are very sorry to say indeed we could not have time to prepare our letter in answer to your letter addressed us under the date of the City of Washington 12th September, 1855, and pack some suitable articles of presents that would be designed to you from us for expression of our being very sincerely gratitude to your kind friendships (sic). . ."[26]

Eventually, after Harris left Bangkok for his mission to Japan, King Mongkut arranged that his elaborate set of gifts to President Pierce be shipped via Singapore. His official Royal Letter contained a very detailed list of these gifts in Thai and English (see Chapter One, Royal Letters).

[26] USNA, Ceremonial Letters, Record Group 59

23

The careful process of choosing gifts, and the huge scale of the Thai Royal Gift, began again when King Chulalongkorn decided to mount a "Siam Exhibit" at the 1876 Centennial Exposition in Philadelphia. This collection, which is both exhibit and gift, was carefully inventoried. During this inventory process, certain items were assigned numbers, which were written on a tiny slip of paper (in Thai) and pasted to the actual item. Then, the number was noted on the inventory. This time-consuming process was abandoned after 83 items. Even John Chandler, the American missionary, teacher, and engineer appointed commissioner of this exhibit by King Chulalongkorn, noted that the collection of over 900 items was crowding him out of his house, where he was supervising the packing.[27]

Thai Royal Gifts to heads of state were carefully chosen from several categories of items normally bestowed upon Thai royalty and nobility by the King. Within Thailand, sets of insignia were given to noble people and royal family members by the king when he bestowed ranks and titles on them. Siam had both a civil nobility of non-royal people with assigned ranks and an extended royal family of all people with inherited royal status, descended from each of the Chakri dynasty kings. Both noble and royal positions of status in the Thai hierarchical social system were assigned points or degrees of *sakdina*, literally, the right to rule over certain grants of land.[28]

Sets of insignia included several categories of objects, most commonly betel sets, textiles, mother-of-pearl inlay vessels, musical instruments and royal drums, weapons, umbrellas of office, and some type of transportation. There were three basic levels of insignia of rank in Thailand in the nineteenth century; those of the king, those of the royal family, and those of the nobility. The highest ranking person in the court was, of course, the king. Power of kingship was associated with the ownership of special exclusively kingly regalia, such as Weapons of Sovereignty and Royal Insignia.[29]

These insignia sets were made up of prestige items, many of which have their symbolic origins in ancient courts. Prestige items from other Asian courts were often taken on by the Thai court and added to the extensive patrimony of symbols of rank for the king, his family members, and high-ranking princes. Although most of the insignia of rank of the Thai court are symbols from other ancient South Asian, Southeast Asian, and East Asian courts, they are used and sometimes manufactured in a distinctively Thai fashion.[30] Manufacture of prestige items in Thailand was controlled by the crown. Each type of craft had its own department in the government, known as a "*krom*" where each group of artists was supervised by a prince. Prestige items were amassed by the court through the gift exchange and tribute system and redistributed in a highly ritualized manner, both within and outside of the Thai kingdom. This complex system of gift exchange was therefore a major catalyst in Thai economic and artistic life.

4. ROYAL REQUESTS AND WESTERN GIFTS

For the most part, Western powers wished to reciprocate Thai Royal Gifts. During the reign of King Rama III, high-ranking members of the Thai Court (especially the Bunnak family) Prince Mongkut (later King Mongkut, Rama IV), and his brother, Phra Pin Klao (later "Second King") had received a steady supply of scientific books and equipment from Western missionaries in Thailand who acquired these things on their behalf, and from Western heads of state. Rama III had remained outside of this system and seemed wary of any Western contact. However, with the 1833 treaty came a request for many Western items for the King and im-

[27] USNA RG 59, Consular Dispatches, 1876.

[28] McFarland 1944 p. 792

[29] The regalia and insignia of the king are described and illustrated in Wales 1931, p. 92; Brus 1985 ; and in Krairiksh ed, et al 1985, Vol. 1.

[30] Wales 1931, pp. 92-116 speculates on the Indic origins of Thai kingship and on the Brahmanic and animist power amassed by ancient kings. Jessup 1990, pp. 89 and 96 discusses the spiritual nature of regalia and insignia of rank. Wilson 1970, pp. 470-474 illuminates the aspect of the Thai king as power broker. This situation of the Thai King as the sole node of royal power (with support from the nobility, not other royal family members) was reinforced by Rama II with a re-shuffling of the nobility that excluded many rival princely relatives and their family lines and brought new allied families into the Sakdina system (Rabibhadana 1969).

◄◄ PRESIDENT ANDREW JACKSON
Term of Office 1829-1837
Library of Congress, Prints and Photographs
Neg. # Z62-50466

PRESIDENT FRANKLIN PIERCE
Term of Office 1853-1857
Collection of the author

◄◄ PRESIDENT JAMES BUCHANAN
Term of Office 1857-1861
Library of Congress, Prints and Photographs
Neg. # Z62-415

PRESIDENT ABRAHAM LINCOLN
Term of Office 1861-1865 (assasinated)
Library of Congress, Prints and Photographs
Neg # Z62-95719

portant members of the court. This was a good opportunity for the scholarly royalty and nobility of Thailand to improve their knowledge of Western science and
culture. For this reason, American and Western diplomatic gifts to Thailand look
musty and rarified compared to the luxurious and beautiful gifts of the Thai court;
however, they represent the most up-to-date scientific information of their day,
and indeed helped the Thais to launch themselves on a self-determined path to the
future.

While foreign heads of state and envoys were motivated for the most part by
trade issues, the Thai court wished to develop strong alliances with the West while
still maintaining sovereignty. Despite these crosscurrents, genuine friendships developed between the Kings, the heads of state, and the envoys. Western heads of
state sincerely wished to please the kings with proper and useful gifts, and the
kings took this opportunity to make special requests of emissaries and heads of
state. In 1821 King Rama II requested armaments, but since Britain was heavily involved in Burma, John Crawfurd was forced to ignore this request. The beautiful
white horse that he brought for the king, however, was the first gift to leave Crawfurd's ship.[31]

During Roberts' mission of 1833, he was given a list of requests:

"The Minister of Foreign Affairs requested the following:

For the King:

5 pairs of stone statues of men and women – some of the natural and some of larger life (i.e., some lifesize, some larger than life) – clothed in various costumes of the United States.

10 pairs of vase-lamps

1 pair of swords – with gold hilts and scabbards – to be of gold, not gilt. Shape of blade a little curved."[32]

The design of the sword was left up to the Americans, who later presented the King with the famous "Eagle and Elephant" sword – with an elephant on the hilt and an eagle on the scabbard – that has become an emblem of United States-Thai relations.[33] This sword is kept and frequently displayed in the Grand Palace in Bangkok. King Mongkut showed Townsend Harris and his American delegation this sword during their formal audience.[34] Ship's Surgeon Dr. Wood was at his side and observed " The king then went on with quite a long history of the various embassies which had visited Siam, and held up a gold-scabbard sword which had been presented through Mr. Roberts to the then king, and had fallen to him. He seemed to prize it highly."[35] Many of these gifts and others like them are displayed in the Royal Palace in Bangkok today.

It is fortunate for the Thais that they began to supply the Americans with suggestions for gifts, because, left to their own devices, the U.S. envoys (usually responsible for choosing gifts if the American government had neglected to) came up with ghastly choices. In Edmund Roberts' case, he was forced into this situation because the President's shipment had been lost.

Before Sir John Bowring left Bangkok in April of 1855, King Mongkut outlined his requests:

"The king said he should like to have astronomical and philosophical instruments, models of engines, a good telescope, an armillary sphere, a model of a screw-steamer, a code of signals, a hydrometer, a ventometer, and specimens of the most approved instruments of war, such as muskets, pistols, swords, etc."[36]

The perils of 19th-century shipping caused damage many times in Thai-Western gift exchange. Perhaps the most tragic situation was in 1856 when the British shipment of expensive scientific devices (globes, cameras, books, and charts) which Bowring had so carefully arranged, sank aboard a small boat which was in the process of ferrying the gifts to the *HMS Aukland*, a steamship that was to take them and British envoy Harry Parkes to Bangkok to ratify the 1855 British treaty.[37]

As if he had read this very list, on his way to Asia in 1855, Townsend Harris, American "Minister Plenipotentiary" and Consul to Japan who was sent to Siam to negotiate a Treaty of Friendship and Commerce, bought in London a set of books, maps, scientific instruments (a microscope and prepared slides for King Mongkut, and an electrical machine and set of electrical experiments for Phra Pin Klao), mirrors, chandeliers, and prints of views of the United States for both rulers.

Townsend Harris was very concerned about the safe-keeping of these gifts during the voyage and took very good care of them; he was especially worried about the mirrors and chandeliers when the *USS San Jacinto* fired its cannons in a 21-gun salute to the king. However, return gifts sent in 1857 from America did not fare as well. In 1859 John Chandler, U.S. Consul at the time, sent a long and detailed letter to President James Buchanan about his embarrassment over the poor treatment of return gifts sent by the U.S. to the King in 1857, mostly consisting of books that, because of poor packing, had become damaged on their journey.

[32] Roberts, 1833, Diplomatic Records, RG 59, U. S. National Archives

[33] See Bhongbhibat 1987 for a history of U.S.-Thai relations "The Eagle and the Elephant"

[34] U.S. National Archives, RG 59 Consular Dispatches, 1833, E. Roberts. Bhongbhibat et al 1982 chronicles and comments upon the history of Thai American relations. Harris describes the moment when King Mongkut brought out the sword for him to see. Cosenza 1930 p. 133.

[35] Wood 1859, p. 206.

[36] Bowring 1857, p. 323

[37] Moffat 1961, p. 192. Shipwrecks and the vagaries of ocean travel plagued diplomatic missions. Because of lack of fuel, the San Jacinto, which was to meet Townsend Harris in Singapore, had to travel under sail rather than steam and therefore was weeks late getting to port. This held up the Harris mission and explains his general restlessness in Siam, which was to be a brief stop for him on the way to his post as U.S. Minister and Consul to Japan (Wood 1859).

5. CHRONOLOGY OF THAI ROYAL GIFTS TO THE UNITED STATES OF AMERICA

THE TREATY OF AMITY AND COMMERCE, 1833

In 1833, the Treaty of Friendship and Commerce between Thailand and the United States of America was written in Thai, Portugese, Chinese, and English. It included the seals of each major Thai government official, King Rama III, and U.S. Special Envoy Edmund Roberts. (Detail)

After the fall of Ayutthaya in 1767, a new dynasty, the Chakri Dynasty, was begun by King Buddha Yot Fa Chulalok Maharaj, Rama I, in the new royal capital of Rattanakosin (Bangkok), on the left bank of the *Menam Chao Phraya* (Chao Phraya River).[38] the next significant contact between Siam and Western powers was in Bangkok during the reign of King Buddha Loet La Naphalai, Rama II (r. 1809-1824). At that time Western powers, active in Java, Burma, China, and Vietnam, were pushing the Thai court for trade agreements, hoping to open new markets for western goods and to gain access to Asia's rich natural and agricultural resources.[39] King Buddha Loet La Naphalai, Rama II, received an envoy from the Portuguese in 1820, and trade with the West resumed in a small way. Britain's East India Company sent an envoy, John Crawfurd, in 1821, but he failed to conclude a treaty.

The first official American contact with Thailand (Siam) came in the Reign of King Nang Klao, Rama III (r. 1824-1851). Following on the heels of Burney's successful 1829 British mission to Siam, American special agent Edmund Roberts arrived in Siam in February 1833 aboard the frigate *USS Peacock*. His mission was to negotiate a treaty of friendship and commerce. The exchange of gifts of state was an important part of such missions, and Edmund Roberts prepared the American gifts carefully. Unfortunately, due to the delay of the ship carrying the gifts of the President, the *Peacock* was forced to leave port without the official gifts and he had to settle for giving the king inferior trade goods from China, while waiting for the official gifts. Roberts in turn received a gift on behalf of the US that was strange to him, a collection of riches from the rain forests of Thailand, a gift that he summarily dismissed in his journal.

[38] Rattanakosin has remained the Thai capital even as it was renamed Krungthep Mahanakorn, etc. (The Great City of the Angels, etc.) in the Fifth Reign. Its name became fixed in the Western world as Bangkok, which retains that use to the present. In this book, Bangkok is used throughout.

[39] The Thais insisted that Westerners must pay duty based on the size of their ships. The Westerners were unhappy because this provision did not consider the value (or lack of value) of the cargo (Hodges 1991).

27

BUST OF KING MONGKUT, RAMA IV
Copper plating, plaster, paint
Gift of King Chulalongkorn, 1876
Siam Exhibit, U.S. Centennial Exposition
USNM # 27439 (4003-A)
Height 80.14 cm. × width at shoulders 50.6
cm. × depth of base 20.6 cm.

This painted plaster bust of King Mongkut is a portrait unusually Western in style. King Mongkut's decorations are the Ancient and Auspicious Order of the Nine Gems and the Most Exalted Order of the White Elephant. The years of King Mongkut's reign are painted in English on a label at the base of the bust.

The artist was most probably Phra Ong Chao (Prince) Pradit Warakan, a distinguished sculptor and director of Royal artists in the Royal Arts Guild *Chang Sip Mu.* Prince Pradit created sculptures of all of the past kings of Siam for the Royal Pantheon at the Grand Palace at the order of King Mongkut, Rama IV, a commission he completed during the reign of Rama V.

The norm in the history of Thai art was for artists to remain anonymous and works of art as a rule were not signed. Often these works were collaborative efforts undertaken in service to the King or to other patrons. It is through lists of the *Chang Sip Mu* that the identities of artists can be discovered. Artists' careers can be tracked through these lists. However, in the Thai system of ranks, their personal names were dropped in favor of titles of ranks. Unless specific works are cited in written histories of the court as works of a particular artist, we can only speculate that the artist in charge of the particular medium ultimately designed and directed the work.[40]

---

[40] Kalyanamitra 1977

FIG 6

28

THE 1856 HARRIS TREATY GIFTS

FIG 7

KING MONGKUT AND QUEEN DEBSIRINDRA. 1856.
Gift of King Mongkut, 1856
Harris Treaty Gifts
USNM # 4003 Smithsonian Institution
National Anthropological Archives Neg # 1735

King Mongkut added photographs of himself and members of the Royal Family in his Royal Gifts, a real indication of the personal nature of his contact with Western leaders. Since these photographs contained the likeness of the King, they were wrapped very carefully in luxurious cloth envelopes officially sealed with wax impressed with the Royal Signet, much as the Royal Letters, containing the words of the King, were wrapped, sealed, and transported on a gold salver. (The envelopes sent by King Mongkut and Phra Pin Klao are shown in Figures 24 and 26).

This intimate portrait is unlike many others of the Thai Kings, who are usually shown seated on one of the thrones next to at least part of their regalia. By contrast, here King Mongkut is seen wearing a rather simple outer robe, and is bare-headed, seated next to his queen. Although he is holding a Royal Sword, part of the Royal Regalia, and wearing a gem-studded waist ornament and several rings, none of the other kingly regalia are visible. Presumably his queen is pictured because so many Western leaders had inquired about the status of the major queen among the inner palace of queens and consorts.

Queen Debsirindra (Rambhery Bhamarabhiramy) was King Mongkut's Queen Consort, having gone through the marriage ceremony with the King and having received the Queens title and privileges. She is shown here in the style of mid-nineteenth century Thai court dress, abrush hair cut, artfully plucked eyebrows, wearing a *Pra Pusa*, the Royal equivalent of the traditional Thai skirt, pleated at the waist and held by a belt ornamented with gems. She was the mother of Rama V, King Chulalongkorn, and three other royal children. She died in childbirth in 1861.[41]

---

[41] Chakrabongse 1967, pp. 178-267.

FIG 8

PAIR OF BRASS STANDS
Phan
Gift of Phra Pin Klao, Uparat (Second King),
1856
Harris Treaty Gifts
USNM #s 46, 47
46: 57 cm diameter × 26 cm height
47: 50 cm diameter × 22 cm height

Phra Pin Klao was the younger full brother to King Mongkut, and occupied the post of "Second King",[42] a post created by King Mongkut as a way to balance the political forces that swirled in the court. He lived in a palace that was attached to the front of the Grand Palace grounds, called the Front Palace, or the Wang Na. His main duty was to command the military forces and defend the King and the kingdom. Phra Pin Klao was a connoisseur of all things Western. A great proponent of the Thai navy, he was involved in building the first Thai steamship.

After the 1833 Roberts treaty, the next opportunity for gift exchange with the American president came in 1856 when the United States negotiated a new treaty with King Mongkut, Rama IV. A rather free-thinking scholar and scientist, King Mongkut had been a monk for twenty-seven years during the reign of his predecessor, Rama III. King Mongkut's familiarity with Western ideas invigorated the Thai relationship with the West, and a flurry of new treaties were signed during the early years of his reign. The new Thai-American treaty, known as the Harris Treaty, was named for U.S. Envoy Townsend Harris, the colorful, bombastic diplomat who was in a hurry to get to his new post as the first American Consul General and Minister to Japan.[43]

The United States was in a very strong position to become an important ally to the Thais, as America had no designs on the sovereignty of any Southeast Asian nation, at least at that time. Although actual treaty negotiations were delayed by a month while the Thais and envoy Harry Parkes finished ratifying Bowring's 1855 British treaty, once that treaty was finished it became the basis for the American treaty, and Harris had only to negotiate minor points.

---

[42] The highest ranking prince was traditionally appointed Uparat. King Mongkut revived the ancient Thai position of the "Second King," and gave his brother Phra Pin Klao equal *sakdina* rank to his own, but as mentioned earlier, his responsibilities were to the military defense of the king. This dual governance allowed a balance of power in the Fourth Reign along complex political and family lines (Chakrabongse 1967, pp 184-85; Rabibhandana 1969, pp 54-66).

[43] Townsend Harris's and King Mongkut's versions of these same events detail the striking contrast of the Thai and American cultural norms of the times. See Cosenza 1930 and U.S. National Archives, Ceremonial Letters, 1856, King Mongkut.

Harris's speeches to King Mongkut and Phra Pin Klao sum up the American position:

"Siam produces many things which cannot be grown in the United States, and the Americans will gladly exchange their products, their gold and their silver for the surplus produce of Siam. A commerce so conducted will be beneficial to both nations, and will increase the friendship happily existing between them".[44]

Harris went on to elaborate on this position in his formal audience with the Second King, Phra Pin Klao, the next day:

"The United States does not hold any posessions in the East, nor does it desire any. The form of government forbids the holding of colonies. The United States therefore cannot be an object of jealousy to any Eastern Power. Peaceful commercial relations, which give as well as receive benefits, is what the President wishes to establish with Siam, and such is the object of my mission".[45]

The tone of the American visit was festive, for the United States Government had supplied Harris with a military band, which was employed often by the Americans for both ceremonial and social events. The presents from the American President needed to be conveyed up the river to Bangkok in "The Royal Seat of Siamese Naval Force" a steamer, painted "bright blue" according to Wood, assembled by a set of Thai noblemen and princes from an American engine, with assistance from some American residents of Bangkok. A set of royal escort barges with the American Marine Guard unit aboard preceeded the steamer, and as the presents were conveyed up the river towards Paknam, the band played "Hail Columbia", and switched to "God Save the Queen" as they passed by the *HMS Saracen*.

Later, on May 1st, the gifts to King Mongkut from President Franklin Pierce were brought up in a procession to the landing at the Grand Palace.[46] Ship's surgeon Dr. Wood gives a thorough account of the procedure:

". . .about twelve o'clock we started from our quarters in the large state barges that the king had sent for us. First went the boats containing the band; then followed the boat with the President's letter, which was deposited upon an elevated and canopied throne. . . .the letter itself was laid out in a portfolio of embossed purple velvet; heavy white silk cords attached the seal, which was shut in a silver box ornamented with the relief of the arms of the United States. The cords passing through the seal and box were terminated by two heavy white silk-cord tassles; the whole was enclosed in a box in the form of a book bound in purple and gold; over this was thrown a cover of yellow satin. The marine guard, in two boats under the command of Lieutenant Tyler, escorted that containing the letter. Next came a richly-canopied and curtained boat containing specimens of the presents from the United States to the king. This was followed by the barge containing the commissioner [Townsend Harris], his interpreter, Rev. Mr. Mattoon, and his secretary, Mr. Heuskin, with one of the ship's coxswains carrying the United States flag. The Commodore, his secretary and I occupied the next boat; and then followed the remaining officers of the suite. . .the whole procession must have extended along the river for at least half a mile".[47]

[44] Harris 1930, p. 134. Speech given at the first audience with King Mongkut, May 1, 1856.

[45] Harris 1930, p. 135-6. May 2, 1856.

[46] Chandler carried on a running commentary to the State Department and to Presidents Pierce, Buchanan, and Lincoln about the importance of learning and respecting Thai court traditions, given the importance of American relations with Siam. U.S. National Archives RG 59, Consular Dispatches, 1856-1864, J. Chandler.

[47] Wood 1859, p. 201-202.

To

Franklin Pierce President
of United States of America
&c   &c   &c

พระบาท   สมเด็จพระ

ปรเมนทรมหามกุฎ   พระ

จอมเกล้าเจ้าอยู่หัว ทรงยินดี

THE STATUS AND RANK OF THE PRESIDENT OF THE UNITED STATES

All of the European monarchs and states had been put on an equal footing with the Thai court, as evidenced by the Royal level of gifts sent to Queen Victoria, and to France. In the past, the Thai court had sent a "Gift of Respect" to the United States. But what to do with the President of the United States, an elected official in a democratic country? This was a great matter for consideration during the negotiations for the Harris Treaty of 1857. King Mongkut had apparently rejected the thought of sending another "Gift of Respect". But what level of gift should be sent at the conclusion of the Treaty negotiations?

King Mongkut decided that the President of the United States is not quite a monarch, but as the head of state, he should receive a Royal Letter along with the insignia of rank of a very high nobleman,[48] rather than the insignia of a king's rank. In contrast, gifts to Western Monarchs were the equivalent of the jewel-encrusted posessions of Royal Family members. King Mongkut and his brother, Phra Pin Klao who was simultaneously a reigning Upparat (the Second King), each sent sets of gifts to President Pierce.

Phra Pin Klao's gift was the more traditional of the two. He sent "elegant and costly specimens of Siamese Garments. . ., silverware plated with gold. . ., 1 Brass Drum, 1 Brass Gong, and 2 Brass Stands." The categories represented here are textiles, nielloware betel set, gongs and offering stands (brass instead of pearl-inlay lacquerware).[49]

King Mongkut sent a sword, a kris, a spear, two pairs of gold and silver spears, a tonsure scissors, a pipe and snuff box, a gold snuff box, a cat's-eye ring, golden pocket inkstand, a nielloware betel set of five pieces, "Japanese Vases" or the pearl inlay lacquerware *ta lum*, a Siamese drum, a pair of long drums, two pieces of gilt silk cloth, and four Khmer silk cloths.

King Mongkut added two very Western things, a long, chatty letter in English (a great contrast to the formal Thai Royal Letter), and a photograph of himself and his Queen. The major part of this gift is the traditional *kru'ang yot*. The personal items added on–snuff boxes, pipe, inkstand, ring–are all not traditionally included in these *kru'ang yot* gifts, though they are of value in everyday Western life of the nineteenth century.

King Mongkut's gifts and letters were entrusted to the Rev. Stephen Mattoon, a longtime missionary in Siam, who, since being named the first U.S. Consul to Siam, felt that he should return home to the United States for instructions. Phra Pin Klao's four crates of gifts did go aboard the *San Jacinto*.

---

[48] The American missionary and U.S. Consul John Chandler, also a trusted advisor to the court, describes King Mongkut's decision-making process in this matter. U.S. National Archives, Consular Dispatches 1856, J. Chandler.

[49] U.S. National Archives, Ceremonial Letters, 1856, Phra Pin Klao.

KING MONGKUT'S 1861 GIFTS

Although the timing of insignia gifts was usually associated with the signing of treaties or other important state occasions, from time to time the King could spontaniously send an additional insignia item to complement a set. For instance, perhaps the most famous offer of a gift from a Thai monarch was King Mongkut's 1861 offer of elephants to the United States. The elephants that King Mongkut offered that year to the Emperor of Japan and to the French were readily accepted, and there is evidence that the elephants given to France thrived until at least 1911.[50]

The sword, niello cigarcase, and photograph of King Mongkut and his daughter sent at that time are now stored at the US National Archives.

THAI ROYAL GIFTS AT THE WORLD'S EXPOSITIONS

The first Exposition in which Siam had an exhibit was the Exposition Universelle in 1867 in Paris. The Siam Exhibit there was organized and sent by Rama IV, King Mongkut. This was the first of many expositions in which Siam participated.

Most nations participating in expositions shipped the contents of exposition exhibits back to their home country at the close of the exposition. For Thailand, however, expositions became a new form of Royal Gift, for in most cases the Siam exhibits were given in total to the head of state of the host country, until the late 1880s when Siam established the National Museum. The exhibitor was responsible for shipping the items to the exposition and for staffing the exhibit with commissioners or guides. This exhibit/gift was not attached to any treaty negotiations, it was sent at the request of the host country expressly for the exposition. However, the traditional Royal Gift was the heart of an exposition exhibit. In the case of the Exposition Universelle in Paris, this was a gift of a kingly gold betel insignia set, textiles, weapons, mother-of-pearl inlay lacquerware vessels, and musical instruments.[51] In addition, since expositions were conceived as trade fairs, the Thais sent samples of export articles; chief among these were cotton, tobacco, rice, fish traps (representing their fishing industry) and lumber products. The exposition was a mixed form of gift on the older, redistributive model, but placed firmly in the market economy. It was no longer an exchange in concrete terms, since no exchange gift was given by the host country of the exposition. Nevertheless, one could say that the host country's act of display was the exchange gift, for participation in expositions gave Siam opportunity for further exposure to the marketplace of Europe.

---

[50] See Gereni, 1912.
[51] Grehan, 1870, p. 115-117 describes the Siam Exhibit at the Exposition Universalle.

**PHOTO OF KING CHULALONGKORN,
RAMA V,** on his Second Coronation,
16 October, 1873.
Gift of King Chulalongkorn, 1876
Siam Exhibit, U.S. Centennial Exposition, 1876
NAA Neg. No. 041031.00

King Chulalongkorn, Rama V, is seen resplendent in his gold robes on the day of his Second Coronation. He is wearing the Great Crown of Victory and is surrounded by his other regalia. His father King Mongkut, Rama IV, had died of malaria contracted on an expedition to the Gulf of Siam to observe a solar eclipse (King Mongkut had predicted the solar eclipse precisely) in August, 1868. King Chulalongkorn wrote a touching letter, bordered in black, informing President Andrew Johnson of King Mongkut's death (U.S. National Archives, Ceremonial Letters). King Chulalongkorn also sent these mourning letters to all other Western heads of state at the time of King Mongkut's death. Somdet Chao Phraya Sri Suriyawongse served as regent until King Chulalongkorn's second coronation in 1873 (Chakrabongse 1967; Moffat 1961; Griswold 1960). This daguerrotype was sent along with the Siam Exhibit items for the 1876 Centennial Exposition.

FIG 9

U.S. CENTENNIAL EXPOSITION

These two photographs of King Chulalongkorn, one in traditional dress at the beginning of his reign and the other in Western dress a decade later, illustrate the incredible changes wrought by this truly forward-looking monarch, who, during his 43-year reign, (1868-1910) abolished slavery and created a modern government complete with a reformed education system.[52]

---

[52] Chakrabongse 1967, pp. 216-267. See also Chomchai 1965, for an intimate portrait of King Chulalongkorn's early life and a detailed examination of his political reforms.

34

FIG 10

KING CHULALONGKORN IN 1881 DRESSED IN WESTERN-STYLE UNIFORM.
Gift of King Chulalongkorn, 1881
Harris Treaty Revisions
NAA Neg. # 048391.00

King Chulalongkorn was surrounded from an early age by relatives who were enthusiastic about the West. His father, King Mongkut, Rama IV, and his uncle, Phra Pin Klao, and the regent, Somdet Chao Phraya Borom Maha Sri Suriyawongse (Chuang Bunnak), were avid scholars of Western scientific advances and scientists in their own right. These men befriended, through treaties, gifts, and letters, the leaders of many Western nations, beginning the Thai strategy of openness which ultimately kept Siam free of colonial rule. King Chulalongkorn was the first Thai monarch to travel to the West, visiting Europe in 1897 and 1902, and the Thai royal family became quite close to Czar Nicholas II and his family, as well as the German royal family and the king and queen of Denmark. This uniform and the Thai medals are styled after Western uniforms as part of King Chulalongkorn's general strategy of showing the West that the Thais were a civilized people who deserved their sovereignty. King Chulalongkorn also built an impressive array of sumptuously decorated Western-style buildings at the Grand Palace in Bangkok, where he received many Westerners.[53] The Strategy of showing that Thailand could rule itself worked: unlike all its Southeast Asian neighbours and in spite of massive European pressure, Thailand was never colonized by a European power.

Thailand next participated in the Centennial Exposition of 1876, held in Philadelphia. A massive exhibit of Thai artifacts and manufactured goods– over 900 items– was assembled at a cost of over $96,000 (in 1875 dollars). Again the *krueng yot* composed a part of the gift.

This impressive exhibit also included common everyday items showing the richness of Siamese manufactured and agricultural goods, such as Siamese silk and cotton cloth, household items, clothing, objects relating to animal husbandry, basketry, metal and woodworking tools, artists' painting and sculpting tools, fish traps and other fishing gear, mats, ceramics, and, reminiscent of the "Gift of Respect", samples of exotic woods and mineral ores and agricultural items (including 66 samples of various strains of rice at various stages of rice gestation).[54]

The exhibit included items relating to the Thai traditional arts, religious life, and culture such as Buddhist monk's equipment, the royal heraldic seal, and scale

---

[53] For a beautiful look inside the grounds of the Grand Palace, where the success of King Chulalongkorn's building strategy can be seen nestled among the earlier Thai structures, see Warren 1988.

[54] U.S. Navy, 1876 is an English translation of the original Thai inventory of the 1876 Siam Exhibit at the Centennial Exposition.

SET OF IVORY-HANDLED KNIVES AND ARTIST'S TOOLS.
Ivory, steel, and mammal hair. Wood box lined with red velvet.
Gift of King Chulalongkorn, 1876
Siam Exhibit, Centennial Exposition
USNM # 27390

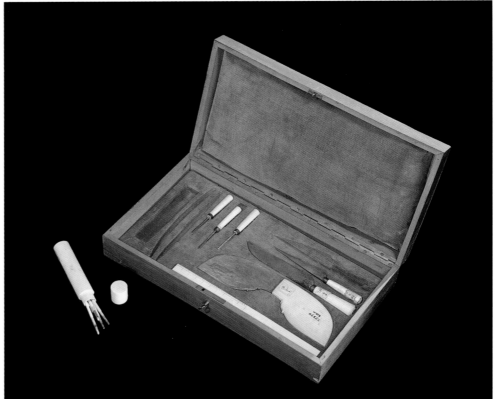

FIG 11

OBJECT LABEL
Siam Exhibit, Centennial Exposition, 1876
USNM # 27181
10.9 cm width × 7.6 cm height

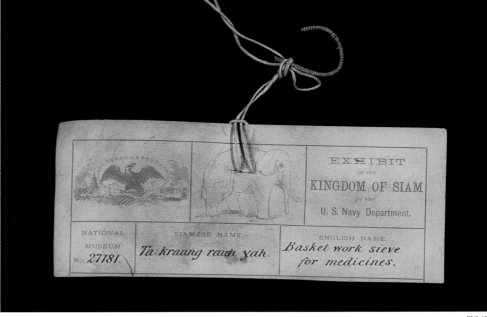

FIG 12

55 The Siam Exhibit of 1876 became a pawn in a power struggle between the original "ugly American," General Frank Partridge the U.S. Consul, and the Thai court, including the former Consul, missionary and tutor of Prince Chulalongkorn, John Chandler. Because of the machinations of Partridge, the Siam Exhibit arrived late. Finally, the U.S. Navy was instructed to go to Bangkok with a gunboat, the *USS Ausheulot*, to retieve the exhibit from Partridge's clutches. The Siam Exhibit finally arrived in Philadelphia in October, 1876, one month before the close of the Centennail Exposition. See McQuail (Taylor) 1991 for the "behind the scenes" story of the Siam Exhibit. U.S. National Archives, RG 59. Partridge, Consular Dispatch #156.

models of the royal funerary chariot and of the magnificent royal barges. There were also leather shadow puppets representing figures from the *Ramakien*–a Thai epic based on the Indian Ramayana–and all of the stages and screens required for a shadow play, or *nang*, along with theatrical or *khon* masks of Ramakien characters. Also included were all of the musical instruments used in such performances. Because of their perishable nature, some of the objects from the Centennial Exposition Siam Exhibit have deteriorated and are no longer in existence, including the tobacco and rice samples as well as the silk Royal Umbrellas. The remaining pieces have been conserved and under study at the Smithsonian since 1989 as part of the "Heritage of Thailand" project.[55]

FIG 13

1904 LOUISIANA PURCHASE EXPOSITION, ST. LOUIS

By the time of the 1904 Louisiana Purchase Exposition in St. Louis, Thailand had established its own National Museum. The Siam Exhibit was much larger than the earlier Centennial Exposition Exhibit, and the Thais even built their own pavilion modeled after Wat Benchamabopit, the Marble Temple, which had just been completed in Bangkok. The important insignia items and the Buddhist objects, theatrical gear and other "high arts" were displayed here in the temple. A fishing exhibit, an exhibit of forest products, wood samples, and agricultural tools and products were displayed in other halls.

The majority of the objects in the 1904 Siam Pavilion were returned to the National Museum in Bangkok. By 1889 the Thai National Museum was well developed and placed under the supervision of the Department of Education. Before that time there were two succesive museums located within the palace walls, the first established by Rama IV, and the second established by Rama V in 1874, and moved outside the palace in 1887 to its present location at the former *Wang Na*, the palace of the Second King.[56] However, ethnological items including hundreds of baskets, fish traps and other fishing gear, models of agricultural implements, and hand-wrought tools from rural areas were given to the Smithsonian Institution at the conclusion of the exposition.[57] Otis Mason, then Head Curator of the Smithsonian's Department of Anthropology, also arranged to purchase twelve Thai baskets. At that time, Mason (an authority on American Indian basketry) was

EXTERIOR, SIAM PAVILION
Louisiana Purchase Exposition, 1904
Library of Congress, Prints and Photographs
Francis Benjamin Johnston Collection
Neg. # LC- Z-62115161

[56] Yupho 1968.

[57] The Siam Exhibit at the Louisiana Purchase Exposition is described in retrospect in Gereni 1912, and the Agricultural specimens and tools in Carter 1904. The author has not as yet located the original Thai inventory for the exhibit. But each piece sent to the Smithsonian had a detailed label, typed in Thai and simple English, describing the piece and its use, and the Thai province of origin. Many of these typed labels as well as individual hand-written paper tags pasted to the objects themselves, are still associated with the tools and implements. The English descriptions on the labels are quite general, but the Thai is very particular. The author is in the process of translating information on the tags to complete the Smithsonian's records for the pieces.

37

FIG 14

SIAM EXHIBIT
Siam Pavilion
Louisiana Purchase Exposition, 1904
Library of Congress, Prints and Photographs
Francis Benjamin Johnston Collection
Neg. # LC-J696-15

SIAM EXHIBIT
Agricultural Hall
Louisiana Purchase Exposition, 1904
Library of Congress, Prints and Photographs
Francis Benjamin Johnston Collection
Neg. # LC-J696-18

FIG 15

FISH TRAPS, MAMMAL TRAPS, AND ZOOLOGICAL SPECIMENS
Agricultural Hall
Louisiana Purchase Exposition, 1904
Library of Congress, Prints and Photographs
Francis Benjamin Johnston Collection
Neg. # LC-J696-21

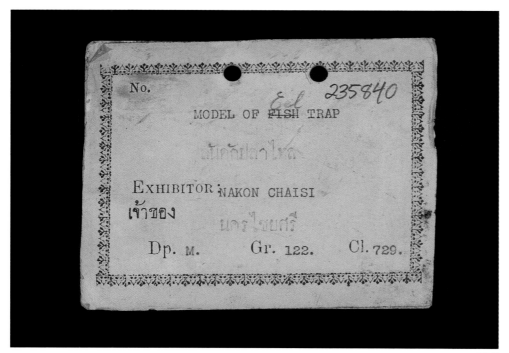

OBJECT LABEL
Louisiana Purchase Exposition, 1904
USNM # 235840 (object label)
10.5 cm width × 8.4 cm height

FIG 18

NORTHERN THAI LACQUERWARE SERVING TRAY
"โต๊ะ *Tok*
Wood, lacquer, and gold leaf
Gift of King Chulalongkorn, 1904
Louisiana Purchase Exposition, Siam Exhibit
USNM # 234041
Height 41 cm. × diameter 18 cm.

NORTHERN THAI LACQUERWARE BOWL ▶
Bamboo, lacquer, and paint
Gift of King Chulalongkorn, 1904
Siam Exhibit, Louisiana Purchase Exposition
USNM # 234040
19.7 cm height × 19 cm diameter

planning a major cross-cultural study of the world's basketry techniques, which he had not completed by the time he died in 1908.

By 1910, the popularity of World Expositions had begun to wane, perhaps because museum exhibits became firmly established as distinct from the trade show business exhibit. Also, like Thailand, many nations were establishing their own national museums and were reluctant to part with important cultural resources that they could house and study themselves. There were no further exposition exhibit items from Thailand deposited at the Smithsonian after 1904. However, even before the 1904 Louisiana Purchase Exposition King Chulalongkorn had learned that Smithsonian staff and other American scholars were keenly interested in using Thai objects in comparative anthropological research, as reflected in pubilcation as well as exhibition. Consequently, he began to send gifts directly to the Smithsonian.

40

FIG 19

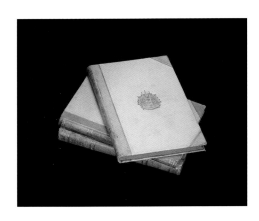

KING CHULALONGKORN'S 1893 VERSION OF THE TRIPITAKA IN THAI
Western-style 33-volume set
Gift of King Chulalongkorn, 1893, to the Smithsonian Institution
25th Year Anniversary of King Chulalongkorn's Accession to the Throne
Smithsonian Institution, Dibner Rare Book Library # PK 4546.A1-1893 RB SI

In 1893, in order to commemorate the twenty-fifth anniversary of King Chulalongkorn's accession to the throne the Royal Press produced this 33 volume Pali version of the Tripitaka in Thai script. This project was started by his father, King Mongkut, in an effort to make the "Three Baskets" of the Buddha's teachings more accessible to Thai readers not versed in the esoteric Pali (Sanskrit-based) script often used for texts. Pali language written in Khmer script was considered the more pure form of the texts for quite some time, but Chulalongkorn's Thai edition contains changes suggested by King Mongkut's scholarship of older Sinhalese (Ceylonese) texts. Sets were sent to major libraries around the world as gifts from the king.

INSTITUTIONAL GIFTS

A new form of Thai Royal Gift–the institutional gift–was developed in the 1880s by King Chulalongkorn. In 1881 the United States and Thailand negotiated changes to the 1857 Harris Treaty. King Chulalongkorn wished to send a gift, but since he had learned that Royal Gifts to the United States presidents had been deposited at the Smithsonian Institution, he planned to send the commemorative gift directly to the Smithsonian. It is interesting that the major part of this gift were "Gift of Respect" or *Khru'ang Ratchabannakan* items, including Gum Benjamin or gambooge (*Styrax benzoin* [*Styracaceae*]) used for skin complaints and rheumatic conditions, *rong thong* (*Garcinia hanburyi*) used as golden-yellow ink in Thailand; Catechu or gambir *sisiat thet* (*Catechu gambir* [*Anacardiaceae*]) used as a masticatory when chewing betel; Cardamom *kra wan* (*Amomum krervanh*, or *Elettaria* sp.) a spice and medicinal remedy; Copal varnish gum *yang* (resinous fuel oil from the tree *Dipterocarpus alatus*); Saltpeter (*din pra siu*); Turmeric (*kamin*); Samrohng seed (*met Samrohng*); *Shoria Robusta* mint seed (*met meng-lak*); lotus seed (*met bua*); the useful medicinal *Nox vomica* (*p'on baa chu*); and rice (*Oryza sativa*). It is possible that in giving this large "Gift of Respect", Thailand hoped to increase trade in these and other valuable items. This was certainly always the goal in giving the historical "Gifts of Respect".

King Chulalongkorn had learned through John Halderman, the U.S. Minister in Bangkok at the time, that the Smithsonian's curators were especially interested in ethnological materials. Therefore, aside from the *Khru'ang Ratchabannakan* trade items, King Chulalongkorn's gift of 1881 consisted of fishtraps and nets, probably from his own extensive royal collections, and the flag of Siam.[58] Although there was a Royal Letter commemorating the treaty negotiations in 1881, it was not connected to the gift in any way, nor does it mention the gifts. The timing of the Royal Gift remained connected to treaty negotiations, but both the content of the gift and the intended receiver of the gift had changed.

King Chulalongkorn sent gifts to allies around the world in commemoration of the 25th anniversary of his coronation. In 1893 the Tripitika, the "Three Baskets" of Buddha's teachings, normally recorded in the Sanskrit-based Pali language script, was printed for the first time in Thai script at the Royal Press. There were no Royal Letters sent out with the books; the volumes were sent directly to institutions of learning throughout the world on behalf of the king through the Siamese Legation office in London (Siam did not have an embassy in Washington until 1901). Multi-volume sets were sent to the Smithsonian Institution, to Harvard University and to Cornell University among others.[59]

During the reign of King Chulalongkorn's son, King Vajiravudh, Rama VI (r. 1910-1925), a set of commentaries on the Tripitaka was printed at the Royal Press in the hopes that it would stimulate the study of Pali scriptures (the set was printed in Thai script). This set, known as the Commentaries of Buddhakosa was complementary to the Tripitaka sent by his father King Chulalongkorn in 1893. In 1927 the set was sent to Cornell University and other institutions in commemoration of the cremation of the late Queen Mother, and in commemoration of the birthday of King Prajadhipok, King Rama VII (r. 1925-1935).

---

[58] Smithsonian Institution Archives, Accession Records, tells of Halderman's discussions with King Chulalongkorn on the topic of the true repository of Royal Gifts in the United States, and the true needs of the Smithsonian Institution at that time.

[59] Accession Records, Cornell University Archives.

RECENT THAI ROYAL GIFTS TO THE UNITED STATES

The role of the Thai Royal Family as desseminators of Buddhist knowledge continues to this day. In the Library of Congress and many other libraries across the United States and around the world, there are housed hundreds of Royal Gifts in the form of volumes of religious works in Thai and Pali.[60]

The present king, King Bhumibol Adulyadej, Rama IX, came to the United States on a State Visit in June of 1960. At that time, he presented the U.S. Library of Congress with an important collection of Thai musical instruments. He also presented President Dwight D. Eisenhower with a teak sculpture of a Thai war elephant. This sculpture is kept at the Eisenhower Presidential Library in Abilene, Kansas. On another State Visit to the United States in 1967, President Lyndon B. Johnson was presented with a beautiful nielloware desk set and a nielloware stand (*phan*), which are in the collections of the Lyndon B. Johnson Presidential Library in Texas.[61]

In 1981 Queen Sirikit donated a collection of Thai basketry to the Smithsonian that are representative pieces from Her SUPPORT Foundation, a program that encourages the maintainence of traditional craftways in Thailand. On the occasion of her visit to the Smithsonian's National Museum of Natural History in 1995, Queen Sirikit also gave the Smithsonian a magnificent model of the Royal Barge *Supannahongse* and a finely detailed embroidery version of a painting done by H.R.H. Princess Maha Chakri Sirindhorn, both created by SUPPORT Foundation artists, as well as some important historic Buddhist manuscripts. This type of Royal Gift serves to turn attention to the people of Thailand and their cultural traditions and to preserve Thai craftmaking traditions.

THE THAI ROYAL GIFTS IN PERSPECTIVE: SYMBOLS OF A LASTING FRIENDSHIP

Thai Royal gifts to America began with very traditional types of gifts, the "Gifts of Welcome", the "Gifts of Respect" *khru'ang Ratchabannakan*, and the *khru'ang yot*, or bestowal of insignia of rank. The *kru'ang yot* gift was very specific as to timing, content, and designated receiver, and was the basis for later elaborations and manifestations of the Thai Royal Gift. Over a 160-year time span, the Thai Royal Gift has changed in every one of its aspects.

The king continues to bestow insignia of rank upon Western heads of state from time to time; however, by the end of King Chulalongkorn's 43-year reign, much of the traditional insignia worn by the king and noblemen at court had been replaced by Western symbols. Western-style military uniforms had for the most part replaced the imported Indian Benares silks; new Western-style medals replaced other insignia; and the power of the king was no longer measured in the number of people, craftsmen and others, whose labor he controlled. The king's power had to confront and become more analagous to a Western power in some respects–the Kings became great benefactors, and prevented colonial encroachment through

---

[60] Letters at the University Archives, Cornell University, and at the Library of Congress document these gifts.
[61] McQuail 1995

FIG 20

SET OF BASKETS
Gift of Queen Sirikit to the Smithsonian
Institution, 1982
USNM #s 421961, 421962, 421963, 421964

Small-scale baskets such as these are a popular product of the SUPPORT Foundation artists, and the small scale makes the fine craftmanship used to make this basket all the more remarkable. The base of these baskets are nailed together with metal nails and sewn to the body and the feet of the baskets, and incorporated into the characteristic "exoskeleton" support

structure so common in Southeast Asian basketry. The lower portion of the basket body is plaited in an upright herringbone pattern, while the upper portion is twined in an unusual double layer. The rim is attached by fitting the warp ends into slots in the underside of the rim, and then it is wrapped and sewn down onto the body of the basket forming a tight fit.

FIG 21

Western-style treaty agreements; the Kingdom gained new wealth from international trade.

Thai Royal Gifts have changed from being part of a tribute-fed redistributive system centered on the court to the type of gift that focuses instead on the role of the Thai court as benefactors of Thai tradition, emphasizing the artistic talents and accomplishments of the people of Thailand.

PORTRAIT OF KING CHULALONGKORN
Siam Pavilion
Louisiana Purchase Exposition, 1904
Library of Congress, Prints and Photographs
Francis Benjamin Johnston Collection
Neg. Z62-115160

45

...mditch Phra Paramendr Maha Mongkut by the blessing of highest Supragency of whole universe the King of Siamese Kingdom and the Sovereign of all interior tributary countries adjacent around in every direction viz. Laos or Shiangs on North Western and Northern; Lao Laws on North and North Eastern; Cambodia from North Eastern to South Eastern; most of

FIG 22A

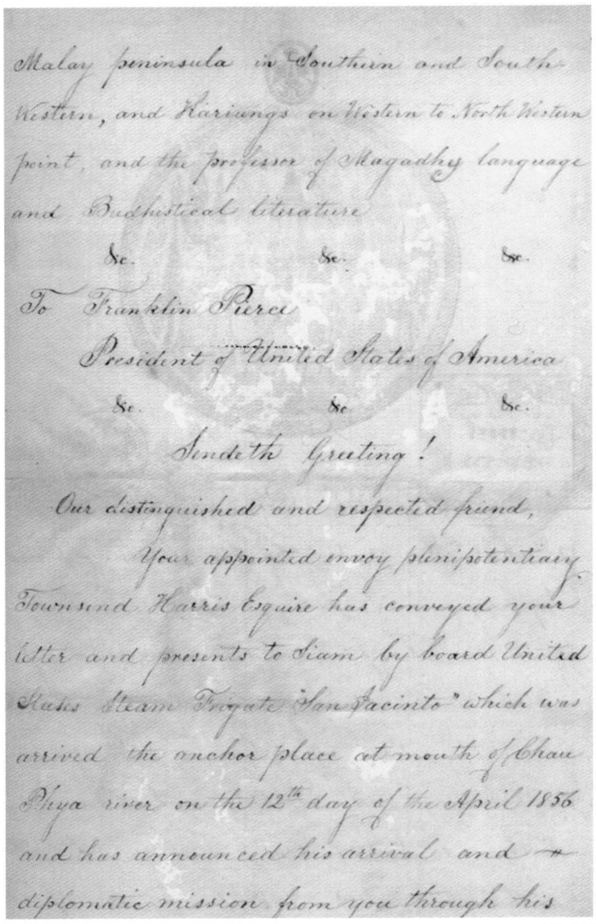

Malay peninsula in Southern and South Western, and Kariangs on Western to North Western point, and the professor of Magadhy language and Buddhistical literature

&c. &c. &c.

To Franklin Pierce
President of United States of America
&c. &c. &c.

Sendeth Greeting!

Our distinguished and respected friend,

Your appointed envoy plenipotentiary Townsend Harris Esquire has conveyed your letter and presents to Siam by board United States Steam Frigate "San Jacinto" which was arrived the anchor place at mouth of Chau Phya river on the 12th day of the April 1856 and has announced his arrival and a diplomatic mission from you through his

FIG 22B

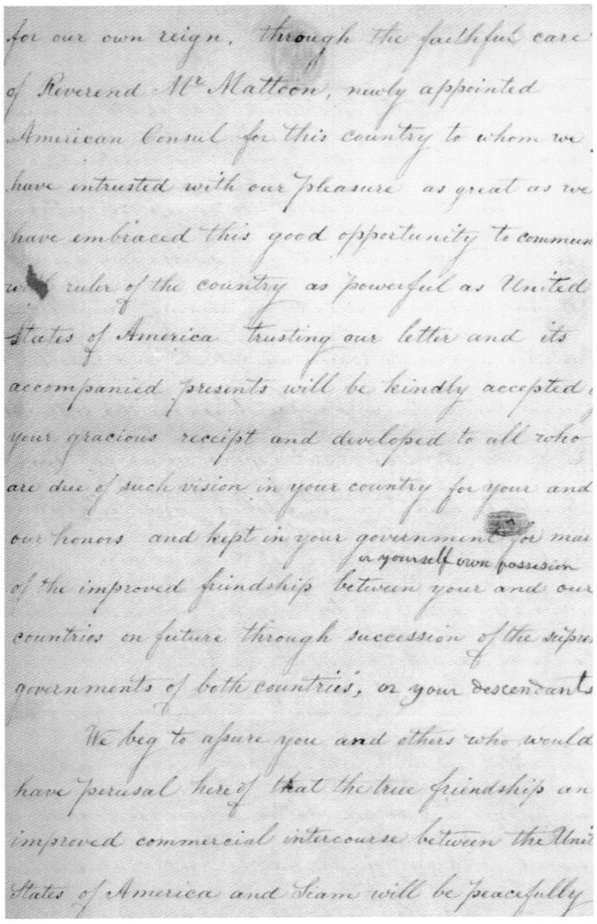

for our own reign, through the faithful care of Reverend Mr Mattoon, newly appointed American Consul for this country to whom we have intrusted with our pleasure as great as we have embraced this good opportunity to commun... ruler of the country as powerful as United States of America trusting our letter and its accompanied presents will be kindly accepted your gracious receipt and developed to all who are due of such vision in your country for your and our honors and kept in your government for mai... yourself own possession of the improved friendship between your and our countries on future through succession of the supe... governments of both countries, or your descendants

We beg to assure you and others who would have perusal hereof that the true friendship an improved commercial intercourse between the United States of America and Siam will be peacefully

FIG 22C

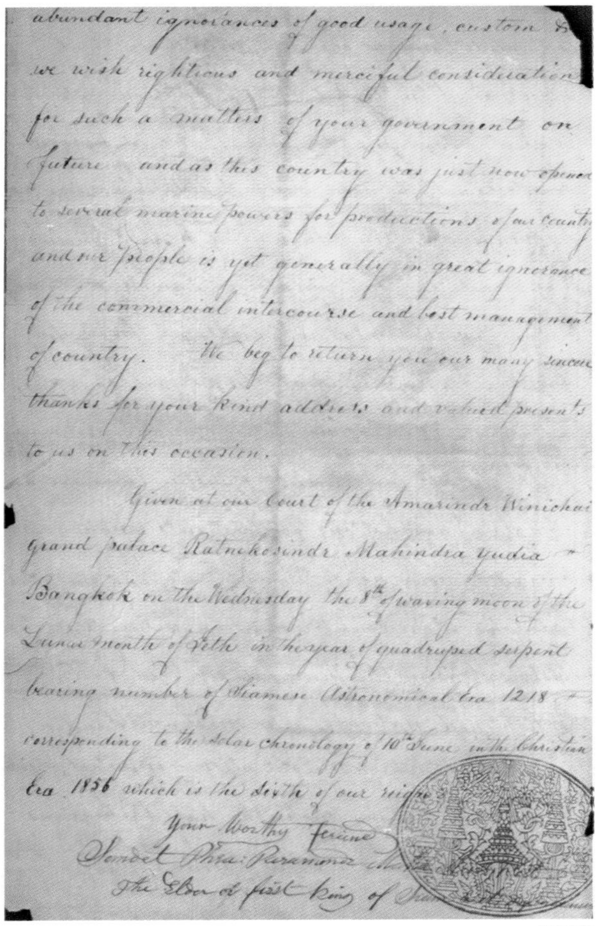

abundant ignorances of good usage, custom ... we wish righteous and merciful consideration for such a matters of your government on future and as this country was just now open... to several marine powers for productions of our country and our people is yet generally in great ignorance of the commercial intercourse and best management of country. We beg to return you our many sincere thanks for your kind address and valued presents to us on this occasion.

Given at our Court of the Amarindr Winichai grand palace Ratnakosindr Mahindra yudia Bangkok on the Wednesday the 8th of waning moon of the Lunar month of Pith in the year of quadruped serpent bearing number of Siamese Astronomical era 1218 corresponding to the Solar chronology of 10th June with Christian era 1856 which is the Sixth of our reign

Your Worthy friend
Sendet Phra Paramendr Maha...
the Elder of first King of Siam...

FIG 22D

46

II CATALOG OF THAI ROYAL GIFTS AT THE SMITHSONIAN INSTITUTION

There are over two thousand Thai Royal Gifts in the Smithsonian Institution's collections. This selection of photographs offers a glimpse of the magnificent quality of court arts and highly skilled ethnological craftwork of Siam. By giving these gifts to America, the Thai kings sealed a lasting friendship between Thailand and the United States which began with the Roberts Treaty negotiations of 1833 and continues to this day, fulfilling King Mongkut's wish which he expressed to President James Buchanan in 1861: "We wish only to confirm the existed [sic] friendship between us and the Government of the United States of America to be remembered for ever."

In these Royal Gifts, the Thai court developed an ancient and widespread Asian courtly gift exchange network to an extraordinary height of sophistication. Asian nations and tributary states had long exchanged embassies and gifts, often in three-year cycles. Even gifts given to him by the King's own Thai subjects were added to the court's cache of potential gifts. These sets of gifts to the U.S. Presidents are no exception; they include items from the Malay States, Japan, China, India, and Indonesia as well as Thailand. They illustrate the extensive geographic reach of the Thai court, as well as the artistry of Thailand's own craftspeople.[62]

In addition to the formal Royal Gifts given by King Mongkut, Phra Pin Klao, and King Chulalongkorn, Thailand also participated in the Centennial Exposition in Philadelphia and the Louisiana Purchase Exposition in St. Louis in 1904. The entire Centennial Exposition Siam Exhibit and the ethnological items from the Louisiana Purchase Exposition were given as a royal gift to the President and people of the United States, and transferred to the Smithsonian with the hope that they would be displayed and shared with the people of the United States and visitors from around the world.

Indeed, over the years, many of these items have been on display in several exhibitions, including a 1976 "Siam" exhibit at the Smithsonian (re-creating part of the 1876 Centennial Exposition); a temporary exhibition called "Royal Gifts from Thailand" at the Smithsonian's National Museum of Natural History in honor of the 1982 Chakri Bicentennial (Bekker 1982), and a 1992 Bangkok and Washington, D.C., traveling exhibition of Thai textiles coinciding with Queen Sirikit's 60th birthday celebrations (Gittinger and Lefferts 1992). In addition, there have been Thai Royal Gifts on long-term exhibit in the Smithsonian's National Museum of Natural History since the 1960s. In 1997, the magnificent sword that King Mongkut gave to President Franklin Pierce (Fig. 85), and a set of gifts given to President Ulysses S. Grant, were on long-term loan display at the Smithsonian's National Museum of American History.

◄ KING MONGKUT'S 10 JUNE 1856 LETTER TO PRESIDENT FRANKLIN PIERCE:
Four pages out of 12. Page 1: Salutation from King Mongkut. Page 2: Addressed to President Franklin Pierce. Page 3: Page with annotated correction by King Mongkut. Page 4: Signature page. U. S. National Archives, RG 59, Ceremonial Letters, Siam.

---

[62] The author presented this material on the meaning of Thai Royal Gifts to America in a slide lecture given at the Smithsonian Institution on October 4th, 1991, at the Seminar in Honor of the Centennial of the Birth of Prince Wan Waitayakorn.

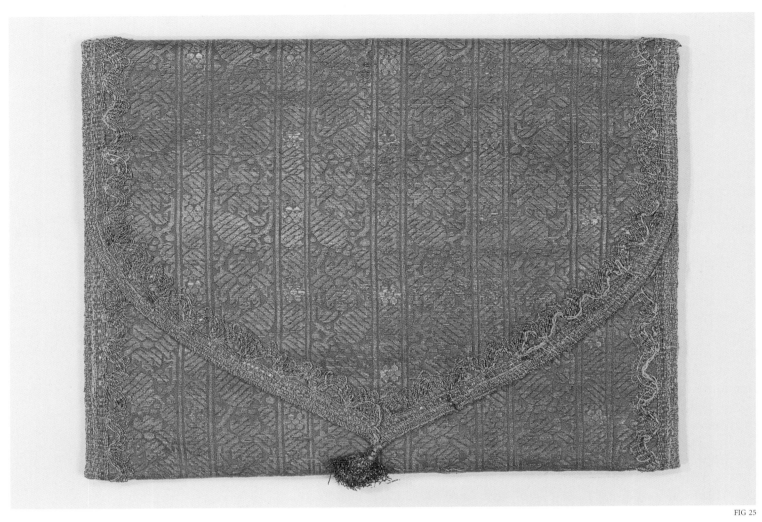

FIG 25

ENVELOPE FOR PHOTOGRAPH OF KING CHULALONGKORN
"กล่องเข็ม"(เข็ม)   *Klong khem*
Gift of King Chulalongkorn, 1876
Siam Exhibit, Centennial Exposition
Indian brocade
USNM # 27275
15.5 cm length × 20 cm width

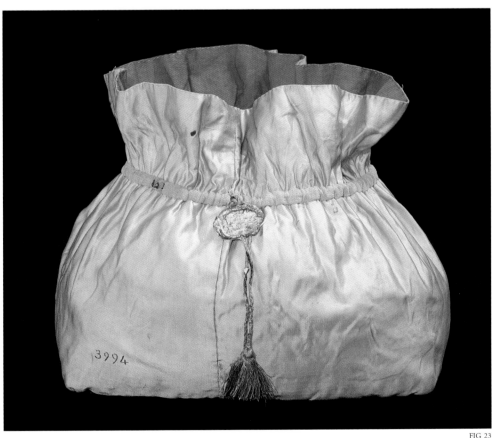

BAG FOR ENCLOSURES
Gift of King Mongkut, 1856
Harris Treaty Gifts
Satin-weave silk
USNM # 49
36 cm length × 29 cm width

FIG 23

48

1. THE ROYAL LETTERS, PHOTOGRAPHS, LISTS OF GIFTS, AND ENVELOPES

Phrarachahattaleka

In the Thai system of divine kingship, the written word of the King was treated as if it were the embodiment of his presence. Therefore, the Royal Letter was, in fact, the most important part of a Royal Gift, for it bore the king's word of intention, signature, and seal. The style of the letter as well as the structure, including preface, body of the letter, a list of gifts and/or a gift of a prayer, the farewell closing statement, and the placement of signatures and seals, and structure and form of the fine textile envelopes,were prescribed by complex court tradition.[63]

It is no wonder that the American "Minister Plenipotentiary" Townsend Harris, upon the conclusion of lengthy treaty negotiations, misunderstood the complexity of the Royal Letter and made the following observation: King Mongkut expressed his regret that since Harris was departing so soon, he had no time to write a letter to the president or to prepare gifts, and sent with Harris instead, according to Harris: ". . . two papers: one a receipt for the [American] presents; and the other an apology for not sending presents and writing a letter to the President, with a short history of the negotiations. The last document must have taken twice as much time as would have sufficed for writing to the President direct."[64] Letters from the Thai Kings, including English translations, were usually written by court scribes, but in the American examples, we see corrections to the scribes' English texts in King Mongkut's own angular writing. The king's corrections to a document were always indicated by a small red seal next to each correction. King Mongkut also wrote separate notes in his own hand to several Western heads of state. He enclosed his calling card and an address card with his gifts to Franklin Pierce.

Thai Royal Letters and letters from heads of state were treated with great deference by the Thais. Phra Wisut Sunton, also known as Kosa Pan, ambassador to the French court in 1685-86, described the proper procedures to be followed with the transport of Royal Letters and the reaction of the French to these measures:

> "Your Majesty's Letter to the French King was brought aboard [the French ship *Oiseau*, bound from Thailand to France] with all due ceremony by my deputy, Your Second Ambassador. Following our custom, Your Royal Letter was in a gold box, inside another bigger silver box, which itself was enclosed in a lacquered wooden casket, wrapped in a rich silk cloth threaded with flowers of gold. It was placed on a gilt throne aloft on the stem of Your Frigate, with many Royal Umbrellas above it. The foreigners are inclined to think that we treat Royal Letters with respect bordering on excess, but since they are an emanation of Your Royal Self, how could we do otherwise than accord the reverence due to Your Person?"[65]

FIG 24

ENVELOPE FOR PHOTOGRAPH OF KING AND QUEEN
Gift of King Mongkut, 1856
Harris Treaty Gifts
Satin-weave silk
USNM # 74
19 cm length × 17 cm width

---

[63] Gallop 1994, p. 13, and pp. 35-101. Gallop's work is a masterful examination of Malay Royal Letters. Thai Royal Letters follow many of the formal patterns described there.

[64] Cosenza 1930. There were three missions in Siam at one time, the French, the British, and the Americans, and it seems as if this severely taxed the manpower and material resources of the Thai court.

[65] Smithies 1990, p. 7.

**ENVELOPE WITH GOLD SEAL OF THE
SECOND KING, PHRA PIN KLAO**
Gift of Phra Pin Klao, 1856
Harris Treaty Gifts
Velvet
USNM # 73
16 cm length × 24.5 cm width

FIG 26

The Thais marked the acceptance of official letters from Heads of State with extreme respect. In this ceremony, in the absence of the sender, the letter was treated as if it were a Head of State. The letter was conveyed in a procession by Royal Barge to the Grand Palace where the King received it and read it. King Mongkut often read the letters aloud, and if they were in French or English, translated the letter into Thai himself for the assembled princes and nobles (Wood 1859, p.206). John Chandler, missionary and second American consul, wrote a detailed letter to President Buchanan describing this tradition and the importance of the State Department supplying appropriate cloth envelopes and sealed presentation boxes for Presidential letters to King Mongkut.[66] These ceremonies were noted by seventeenth century travellers to Ayutthaya and were carried out until 1861, when King Mongkut proclaimed that the processions would cease since with the large volume of correspondence being received from Western heads of state, the commitment of manpower for the complex ceremony, and the din of the cannons that marked each procession were too much for the court to bear.[67]

The blue envelope seen here(USNM # 49) could be the one placed in Townsend Harris' hands by King Mongkut: "He gave me a blue velvet envelope. . .and requested me to open and read [the contents]. There were two papers: one receipt for the presents; and the other an apology for not sending the presents and writing a letter to the President, with a short history of the negotiations."[68]

**CARD ADDRESSED TO PRESIDENT ▶
FRANKLIN PIERCE**
Sent with gifts from King Mongkut, 1856
Harris Treaty Gifts
Paper
USNM # 53
21 cm length x 10.4 cm width

[66] U.S. National Archives, RG59 Consular Dispatches, Chandler 1859, another of Chandler's instructional missives to the State Department and the Presidents.

[67] Processions for letters from heads-of-state, by barge and by land were described in English by many, including Bowring 1857, Townsend Harris (Cosenza 1930), and Chandler, 1859. This ceremony and the Royal Decree that ended it is described in U.S. National Archives, RG59 Consular Dispatches; Chandler 1859; Partridge 1861; Wales 1931; and Moffat 1961, p. 65.

[68] Cosenza 1930, p. 161. Harris could have mistaken satin for velvet, or perhaps if a velvet envelope from King Mongkut existed, it is no longer with the gifts. The velvet envelope, USNM # 73, has the Emblem of Office of Phra Pin Klao.

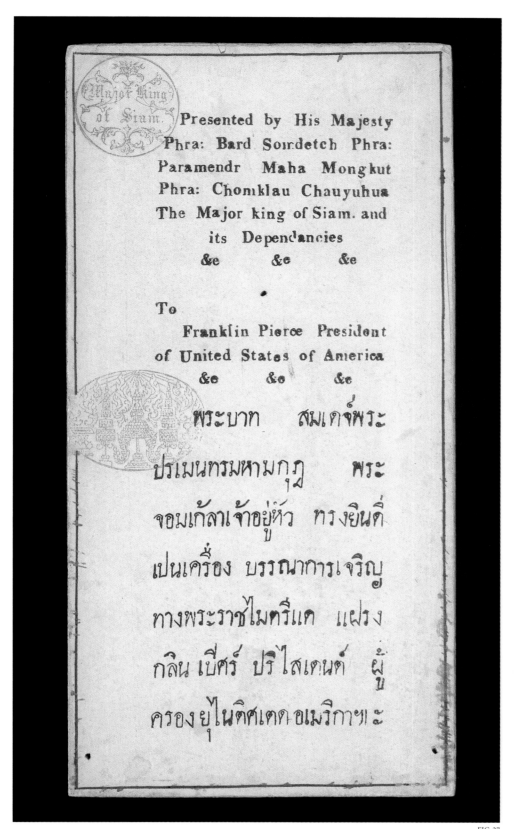

FIG 27

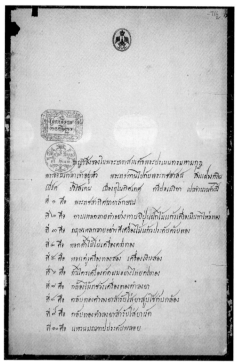

FIG 28A

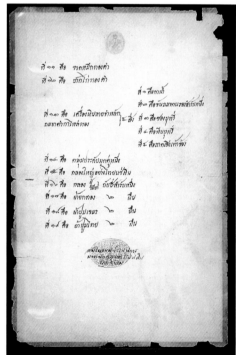

FIG 28B

KING MONGKUT'S THAI LIST OF GIFTS TO THE UNITED STATES, 10 June 1856. U. S. National Archives, RG 59, Ceremonial Letters, Siam.

The gift list shows corrections made in the hand of H.M. King Mongkut, Rama IV (marked by the red seals). These show the King's personal concern with the details of the Royal Gifts sent to the U.S. President.

51

FIG 29

52

2. NIELLOWARE

The craft of nielloware is traditionally thought to have been brought to Thailand in the 16th century by the Portuguese. However, many of the vessel forms in the Smithsonian's collections, particularly the bowl, or *chok*, would seem to indicate a Persian origin. The Portuguese niello tradition was derivative of the Persian tradition, as evidenced by floral and vine motifs on Iberian and Portuguese weaponry of the 16th and 17th centuries. All of the Ratanakosin Period Siamese pieces in the Smithsonian's collections have the intertwined floral patterns seen on 16th Century Safavid-era (1501-1732) Persian pieces, and the water bowls use the same horizontal inscribed lines that divided Persian wine bowls.[69] Certainly, connections made between Siam and the Arab world at the time of Ottoman ruler, Suleiman the Magnificent (r. 1520-1566) by his embassy to Southeast Asia, and the continued Persian mercantile presence, spanning six centuries in the Isthmus of Kra,[70] could explain these similarities in forms. In addition, a southern city visited by the Persians, Nakhon Sri Thammarat, has long been the center for production of nielloware and other metal goods. Other vessel forms and details, such as the shapes of the water pots (kettles used for serving cold water or hot water for tea), seem lifted directly from Chinese tradition. One can see the ceramic influence in the knobs atop the water pots, which are reminiscent of lotus bud knobs on Chinese export ware teapots.[71]

These gold niello pieces are actually gold plated silver which has been shaped and embossed with a heavy relief of designs. The relief is filled in with a black paste alloy of silver, sulphur, and lead. The piece is then sanded and heated (annealed), and the gold plating applied. In fact, the Thai phrase for this type of niello ware is *thom ta thong*, *thom*, meaning "to fill" (with the blackened silver alloy) and *ta thong* "to plate, or electro-plate, with gold." In the past, this plating was accomplished by mixing the gold with mercury. The gold and mercury mixture was applied to the silver, and then heated. At that point, the mercury would evaporate in a poisonous cloud, and the gold plating would adhere firmly to the silver base. The technique of *kru'ang thom*, plain silver nielloware, is sometimes mixed with the *thom ta thong* technique, gold-plated nielloware, to form *thom prak mat*, gold and silver nielloware.

Regardless of its origin, niello is now a classical Thai art, one of the purest expressions of Thai culture. Her Majesty, Queen Sirikit, is today promoting the teaching of the niello craft to young artisans and the marketing of niello in the modern market through her SUPPORT Foundation, as well as commissioning important new works for the court.

◀ RACK FOR HANGING FACE CLOTHS
"ราวแขวนผ้าเชดหน้าถมตะทอง"
(ราวแขวนผ้าเช็ดหน้าถมตะทอง)
Raw khwaen pha chet na thom ta thong
Part of a Toilette Set
Gift of King Chulalongkorn, 1876
Siam Exhibit, Centennial Exposition
Nielloware (silver, silver alloy, and gold)
USNM # 27151
48.5 cm height × 41 cm width × 14 cm diameter at base

---

[69] Melikian-Chirvani 1982, pp. 260-349, see particularly wine-bowl shape of item 163, page 348, and the floral and vine motifs in the body of item 134, p. 304, dated to the late 16th century, A.D. Atil et al 1985 also describes these forms and design motifs.

[70] The adventures of Suleiman's embassy to Asia is recounted in O'Kane 1972. Hall (1985, p. 176), describes the long standing Persian presence in the southern Siamese and Malay peninsula region, with a strong presence in Kedah, later a tributary of Siam, dating as far back as the eleventh century A.D.

[71] Allison (1977) and Graca (1977) document vessel forms and desing motifs of Chinese trade ceramics traded throughout Southeast Asia and Europe by the Dutch East India Company.

BETEL SET WITH ▶
TONSURE SCISSORS
"เครื่องเงินลายจำหลักถมยาดำกาไหล่ทอง"
Khru'ang ngoen lai cham lak thom ya dam ka lai thong

"A SIAMESE HAIR-CUTTING SCISSORS ▶
DIVERSIFIED AND BOTTOMED WITH
GOLD"
"กันไตรเครื่องตัดผมอย่างไทยคร่ำทอง"(กรรไกร)
Kan trai khru'ang tat phom yang thai khram thong
Gift of King Mongkut, 1856
Harris Treaty Gifts
Nielloware (Silver, silver alloy, and gold)
Bowl and stand, USNM # 63; Water Pot,
USNM # 65; Tonsure Scissors, USNM # 66

THE BETEL SET

Use of betel, a mild narcotic, was all-pervasive in nineteenth-century Southeast Asia. Chewing the quid, a combination of the betel-leaf (*Piper betle*) spread with the crushed and liquidized lime catalyst, filled with shredded areca-nut (*Areca catechu*), and sometimes the added resinous masticatory "gambooge" (*Garcinia hanburyi*) and tobacco, produces a mildly narcotic effect and characteristic red saliva. Betel was used and shared on many social occasions.

Betel sets were one of the most visible sign of rank in Thai culture, since bearers carried the sets everywhere behind the noble owners. During Royal audiences, which sometimes stretched on for hours, the sets were spread on the floor surrounding the princes and members of the nobility. The variety of deigns in betel sets reflects the hierarchy of Thai society. All sets sent to the presidents are exactly like insignia of rank made for these high-ranking *Krom* princes and noblemen. As president, these men were important, but they were temporary (though democratically elected) leaders as opposed the the European monarchs, who reigned for life. By contrast, the Kings and Queens of European courts received gold and enamel insignia and regalia fit for Thai Kings, Queens, and *Chao Fa* (children of major Queens).

King Mongkut, Rama IV, included a list of his gifts in both Thai and English along with his set of gifts (see photo of this list, Figures 28A and 28B). It is interesting that the English list is a complex narrative, corrected in King Mongkut's own handwriting, while the Thai list is more straightforward and descriptive. The English description here is King Mongkut's own translation. The Thai is from King Mongkut's Thai list. The set is not complete. There is a possibility that a portion of the set was retained by President Franklin Pierce, since many of these items do not appear on the Smithsonian's initial 1859 inventory.

"Five kinds of silver articles engraved and coloured with metallic black color and richly gilt diversifiedly manufactured by Siamese Goldsmiths,– namely a water pot, a vessel with its standing base, a cigar case, a cigar box, and their plate connected with a stand"
"เครื่องเงินลายจำหลักถมยาดำกาไหล่ทอง" *Khru'ang ngœn lai cham lak thom ya dam ka lai thong.*
"Water pot"
"กาน้ำ" *Ka nam*
"Vessel with its standing base"
"ขันถมพานรองสำรับหนึ่ง" *Khan thom phan rong samrap nu'ng*
"Cigar case"
"ซองบุหรี่" *Song buri*
"Cigar box"
"หีบบุหรี่" *Hip buri*
"Their plate connected with stand"
"ถาดเชิงเท้าช้าง" *That chœng thao chang* (with a base shaped like an elephant's foot)

FIG 30

TONSURE SCISSORS USED IN TOP-KNOT CUTTING CEREMONY:
"A Siamese hair-cutting scissors diversified and bottomed with gold"
"กันไตรเครื่องตัดผมอย่างไทยคร่ำทอง"(กรรไกร)
Kan trai khruang tat phom yang thai khram thong
Gift of King Mongkut, 1856
Harris Treaty Gifts
Nielloware and khram (silver, silver alloy, and gold)
USNM # 66
34.6 cm length × 4.5 cm width

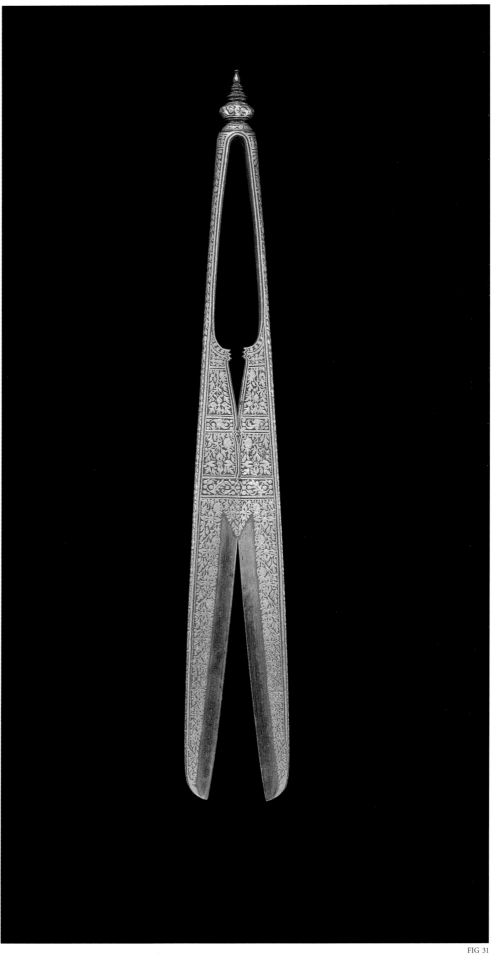

"WATER POT" ▶▶
"กาน้ำ"
Ka nam
Gift of King Mongkut, 1856
Harris Treaty Gifts
Nielloware (silver, silver alloy, and gold)
USNM # 65
18 cm height × 11 cm diameter

FIG 31

FIG 32

57

FIG 33

58

FIG 34

FIG 35

◄◄ **BOWL**
"ขันถม"
Khan thom
Gift of King Mongkut
Harris Treaty Gifts, 1856
Nielloware (silver, silver alloy, and gold)
USNM # 63
10.2 cm height × 21.2 cm diameter

DETAIL, BOWL
"ขันถม"
Khan thom
Detail of lion on bottom
Gift of King Mongkut
Harris Treaty Gifts, 1856
Nielloware (silver, silver alloy, and gold)
USNM # 63

DETAIL, STAND FOR BOWL
"ภานรองสำรับหนึ่ง"(พาน)
Phan rong samrap nung
Gift of King Mongkut
Harris Treaty Gifts, 1856
Nielloware (silver, silver alloy, and gold)
USNM # 63

FIG 36

NIELLO BETEL SET

Gift of Phra Pin Klao, 1856

"SILVER WARE PLATED WITH GOLD"

BETEL SET
"ภานหมากถมตะทองมีเครื่องใน"(พาน)
"Phan mak thom ta thong mi khruang nai"
Gift of Phra Pin Klao, 1856
Harris Treaty Gifts
Nielloware (silver, silver alloy, and gold)
USNM #s 57, 58, 59, 60, 61, 62

At each end:
"2 STANDS, THE RIMS OF THE BOWLS OF WHICH ARE DENTICULATED"
"ภานพักใบเสมา"(พาน)
Phan phak bai sema
USNM # 57, USNM # 58
Both, 14 cm height × 57 cm diameter

Interior pieces, left to right:
"WATERPOT"
See: Fig. 37, right

"STAND, THE RIM OF THE BOWL OF WHICH IS DENTICULATED"
See: Fig. 40, opposite page

"SPITTOON"
"กะโถน"
Kathon
USNM # 62
25.5 cm height × 29 cm diameter

"CYLINDRICAL WATERPOT"
"กาน้ำรูปกระบอก"
Ka nam rup krabok
USNM # 65

"STAND FOR WATERPOT"
See: Fig. 38, opposite page

FIG 37

"STAND FOR WATERPOT" ▶
"ถาดรอง"
That rong
Gift of Phra Pin Klao, 1856
Harris Treaty Gifts
Nielloware (silver, silver alloy, and gold)
USNM # 59
9.5 cm height × 21 cm diameter

FIG 38

"STAND, THE RIM OF THE BOWL OF WHICH IS DENTICULATED"[72] ▶
"ภานพักใบเสมา"(พาน)
Phan phak bai sema
Gift of Phra Pin Klao, 1856
Harris Treaty Gifts
Nielloware (silver, silver alloy, and gold)
USNM # 57
14 cm height × 57 diameter

FIG 39

"STAND, THE RIM OF THE BOWL OF WHICH IS DENTICULATED"
"ภานพักใบฉาบ"(พาน)
Phan phak bai chap
Gift of Phra Pin Klao, 1856
Harris Treaty Gifts
Nielloware (silver, silver alloy, and gold)
USNM # 60
14 cm height × 20 cm diameter ▶

◀ **"WATERPOT"**
"กาน้ำ"
Ka nam
Gift of Phra Pin Klao, 1856
Harris Treaty Gifts
Nielloware (silver, silver alloy, and gold);
gourd-shaped
USNM # 62
Height 20.5 cm × diameter 15 cm.

[72] These trays have denticulated petals shaped like the leaves of the sacred bodhi tree, *bai sema* under which the Buddha was born (McFarland 1944, p. 883).

FIG 40

FIG 41

GIFTS OF KING CHULALONGKORN

TWO GOLD-PLATED NIELLOWARE BETEL SETS
"ภานหมากถมตะทองมีเครื่องใน"(พาน)
Phan mak thom ta thong mi khruang nai
Gift of King Chulalongkorn, 1876
Siam Exhibit, Centennial Exposition
Nielloware (silver, silver alloy, and gold)
USNM #s 27153, 27154, 27155, 27156, 27157, 27158

At each end:
TWO NIELLOWARE BETEL TRAYS
"ภานหมากถมตะทอง"(พาน)
Phan mak thom ta thong
USNM #s 27154, 27158

Resting inside:
TWO TRIANGULAR DISPENSERS FOR BETEL LEAVES
"ซอง"
Song
USNM # 27153
See also: Fig. 42, at right

Interior pieces, left to right:
SMALL GOLD-PLATED NIELLOWARE SPITTOON
"กะโถนถมตะทองเล็ก"(กระโถน)
Kathon thom ta thong lek
USNM # 27156

GOLD-PLATED NIELLOWARE SPITTOON WITH A LARGE, SERRATED MOUTH
See: Fig. 43, opposite page

POT FOR COLD WATER WITH ITS SUPPORTING TRAY
"กาน้ำเยนถมตะทองมีถาดรอง"
(กาน้ำเย็นถมตะทองมีถาดรอง)
Ka nam yen thom ta thong mi that rong
USNM # 27155

ONE TRIANGULAR DISPENSER FOR ▶ BETEL LEAVES
"ซอง" *Song*
Gift of King Chulalongkorn, 1876
Siam Exhibit, Centennial Exposition
Nielloware (silver, silver alloy, and gold)
USNM # 27153
14 cm length × 7.5 cm width at top

FIG 42

FIG 43

**GOLD-PLATED NIELLOWARE SPITTOON,
WITH A LARGE, SERRATED MOUTH**
"กะโถนถมตะทองปากแกรใหญ่"
Kathon thom ta thong pak krae yai
(กระโถนถมตะทองปากแตรใหญ่)
(Kathon thom ta thong pak trae yai)
Gift of King Chulalongkorn, 1876
Siam Exhibit, Centennial Exposition
Nielloware (silver, silver alloy, and gold)
USNM # 27157
20 cm height × 33 cm diameter

FIG 44

TOILETTE SET
"ภานเครื่องแป้งถมตะทอง"(พาน)
Phan khruang paeng thom ta thong
Gift of King Chulalongkorn, 1876
Siam Exhibit, Centennial Exposition
Nielloware (silver, silver alloy, and gold)
USNM #s 27143, 27144, 27148, 27149, 27150,
27151, 27152, 27156

Often, beautiful nielloware toiletry sets are seen in nineteenth-century portraits of high-ranking Thais. These sets are used by both men and women. The small pots are often used for perfume, cosmetics, or betel.[73]

BASIN FOR WASHING THE FACE
"อ่างล้างหน้า"
Ang lang na
Part of a Toilette Set
Gift of King Chulalongkorn
Siam Exhibit, Centennial Exposition
Nielloware (silver, silver alloy, and gold)
USNM # 27148
18 cm height × 28.5 cm diameter

[73] McFarland 1944.

FIG 48

◄ TOILETTE SET

RACK FOR HANGING FACE CLOTH

"ราวแขวนผ้าเช็ดหน้าถมตะทอง"
(ราวแขวนผ้าเช็ดหน้าถมตะทอง)
Raw khwaen pha chet na thom ta thong
USNM # 27151

BASIN FOR WASHING THE FACE
See: Fig. 48, below left

BOWL WITH LID AND STAND

"ขันถมตะทองมีฝาครอบมีภานรอง"(พาน)
Khan thom ta thong mi fa khrop mi phan rong
USNM # 27150

TWO SMALL CUPS
"จอก"
Chok
USNM # 27156
See also: Fig. 46, right

TOILETTE SET WITH STAND AND SIX
CONTAINERS, three with tapering lids
"ภานเครื่องแป้งถมตะทองมีโถปริกทอง"(พาน)
Phan kruang paeng thom ta thong mi tho prik thong
USNM # 2714

BOTTOM, SMALL CUP ►
"จอก"
Chok
Part of a Toilette Set
Gift of King Chulalongkorn, 1876
Siam Exhibit, Centennial Exposition
Nielloware (silver, silver alloy, and gold)
USNM # 27156
4 cm height × 7.5 cm diamter

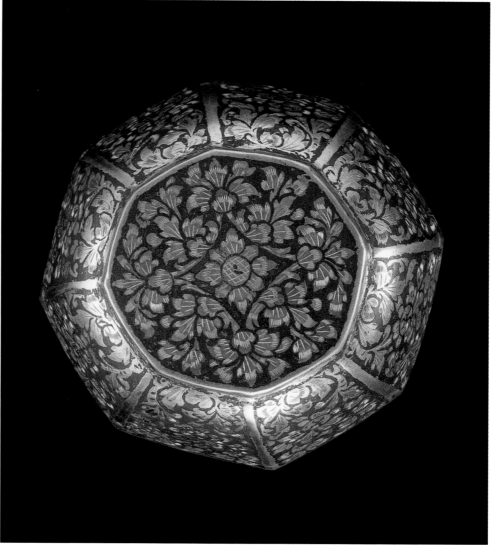

FIG 46

BOWL WITH LID AND STAND
"ขันถมตะทองมีฝาครอบมีภานรอง"(พาน)
Khan thom ta thong mi fa khrop mi phan rong
Part of a Toilette Set
Gift of King Chulalongkorn, 1876
Siam Exhibit, Centennial Exposition
Nielloware (silver, silver alloy, gold)
USNM # 27150
Bowl with cover: 15 cm diameter × 12.5 cm
height
Stand: 9.5 cm height × 14 cm diameter

◄◄ FANCY CONTAINER WITH
TAPERING LID
"โถปริกทอง"
Tho prik thong
Part of a Toilette Set
Gift of King Chulalongkorn, 1876
Siam Exhibit, Centennial Exposition
Nielloware (silver, silver alloy, and gold)
USNM # 27149
8.5 cm height × 6.5 cm diameter

FIG 45

FIG 47

FIG 49

3. BUDDHIST ARTS

Buddhism and Kingship

Thai Buddhist arts were created by artists skilled in plaster work, lacquer work, manuscript painting and calligraphy, and many other arts. Their works were sponsored by the kings and other benefactors of the Thai Buddhist temples.

In Thailand, the relationship between the Buddhist *Sangha* (monkhood) and the court is synergistic. The king is considered defender of the Buddhist faith (and now all other faiths in Thailand), and the *Sangha* is the sanctifier of the king, who is ushered into kinghood through the Buddhist and Brahman ritual of coronation. Monkhood serves as an other-worldy refuge from the restrictive pressures of the Thai social system's hierarchy. All Thai men, including princes and kings, are encouraged to become ordained and serve as monks for at least one three-month period, and many women serve as nuns.

When his elder half-brother was declared King Rama III in his place, Prince Mongkut was serving in the monkhood where he remained for twenty-seven years, using the opportunity to study *Dhamma* (Buddhist doctrine) and reform the entire face of Theravada Buddhism. Upon the death of Rama III, Mongkut the abbot became King Mongkut, Rama IV.[74]

Even a king must make merit and donate gifts and good works. The king's role as defender of the faith (now extended to all faiths in Thailand) is demonstrated in many symbolic ways. Insignia sets awarded by the king always included pearl inlaid *ta lum*, raised trays used to present offerings to monks and in many religious ceremonies, such as weddings, an unspoken intonement that the recipient support the *Sangha*, perhaps. The king himself plays a key role in the Buddhist *Sangha*, bestowing ranks upon the highest-level monks, choosing the Supreme Patriarch, presenting monks with priestly insignia, and delivering robes to monks at certain Royal temples on *Kathin Luang* at the end of the Buddhist Lent. The king has often been the chief benefactor of the *Sangha*; many kings expended much time and effort in building and restoring temples, creating schools within temples, and casting new Buddha figures.

In the nineteenth-century the kings had the opportunity to expand their role of proselytizers of Buddhism and religious tolerance to the West. King Mongkut communicated his message of religious tolerance by allowing Christian missionaries to work in Thailand, and to world leaders in his letters to them. To Pope Pious IX in 1861, he wrote: "For inasmuch as it is difficult to foretell the shape of the life to come hereafter, it is only just to allow every person the right to seek happiness therein in his own way."[76] Carrying on this tradition, King Chulalongkorn finished a publication effort begun by his father years before, and printed the entire *Tripitaka*, the Buddhist canon, in Thai script in time for the 25th anniversary of his accession to the throne in 1893, in both manuscript and Western book format, which he distributed to libraries around the world.

Buddhist arts and texts were almost always included as a part of a Royal Gift. Pearl inlaid *ta lum* offering bowls, buddhist manuscripts and boxes and cabinets to hold them, paintings or models of important temples, and monk's implements such as the prayer fan are all found in nineteenth century inventories of Thai Royal Gifts to the United States.

◄ **MODEL OF** *PUTTHA PRANG*
Wat Arun
Gift of State, 1966
Molded plaster, painted
USNM # 158471
91.5 cm height × 91.5 cm width × 91.5 cm depth of base

Wat Arun Rajawararam, "The Temple of the Dawn", was given this name because it sits to the east, across the Menam Chao Phraya (Chao Phraya River) from the Grand Palace in the city of Thonburi. The founder of the Chakri Dynasty, King Rama I, established the Grand Palace and the City of Bangkok across the River from the Thonburi Palace of the former King Taksin (r. 1767-1782). The future King Rama II (r. 1809-1824) son of Rama I, renovated this temple. He changed its name to *Wat Arun Rajawararam* when he came to the throne and continued to make extensive renovations to it throughout his reign. King Rama III (r. 1824-1851) continued these renovations and completed the construction of the *Puttha Prang* which is a distinguishing landmark of the site.[75]

---

[74] Rabibhadana (1969, p. 122-124), Griswold (1960), Moffat (1961), Wilson (1970) all describe Prince Mongkut's extraordinary life in the monkhood and his emergence as King Mongkut twenty-seven years later.
[75] Burhibad and Griswold 1968.
[76] Moffat 1961, p. 160.

PRAYER FAN
"ตาละปัต"(ตาลปัตร)
Ta la pat
Ivory, silk, and gold threads
Gift of King Chulalongkorn, 1876
Siam Exhibit, Centennial Exposition
USNM # 27267

This *Ta la pat*, or prayer fan was given to high-ranking monks on the occasion of Rama V's second coronation in 1873. King Chulalongkorn's title floats above the Great Crown of Victory, which is displayed between the Royal Umbrellas. Erawan, the three-headed elephant mount of Indra, the Hindu deity is flanked by two *Singhas*, royal lions. The date of King Chulalongkorn's Second Coronation floats on the ribbon above the tapering brace of the ivory handle, on which again is a carving of the Great Crown of Victory and the Royal Umbrellas. The three-headed elephant is a reference to Siam Prathet comprising the three regions of Siam–North, Central, and South. It is flanked by *Gajasri* (Elephantine Lion) and Rajasri (King of Lions). The *Gajasri* represents the might of military authorities, the *Rajasri* represents the might of the civil authorities. Both join together in upholding the Thai Kingdom.

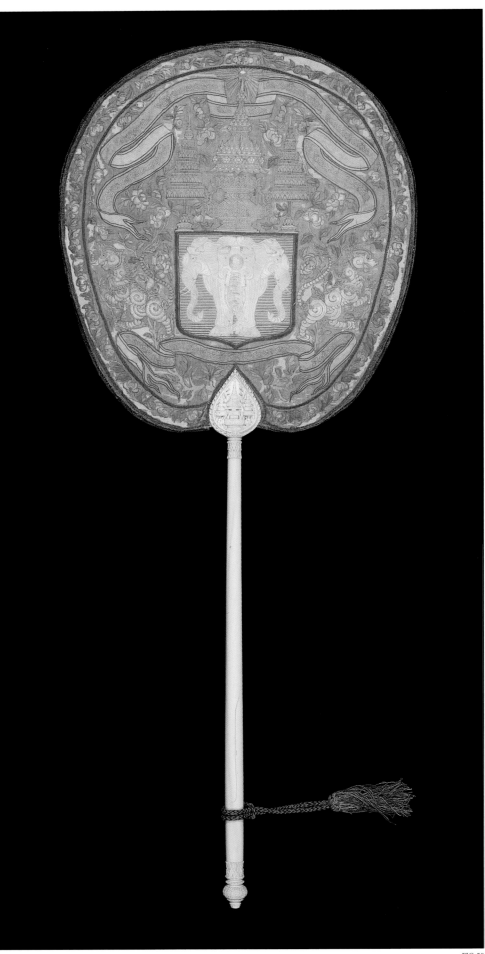

PRAYER FAN, DETAIL OF IVORY HANDLE ▶
"ตาละปัต"(ตาลปัตร)
Ta la pat
Ivory, silk, and gold threads
Gift of King Chulalongkorn, 1876
Siam Exhibit, Centennial Exposition
USNM # 27267
98 cm length × 40 cm width

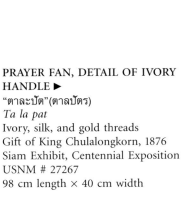

FIG 50

68

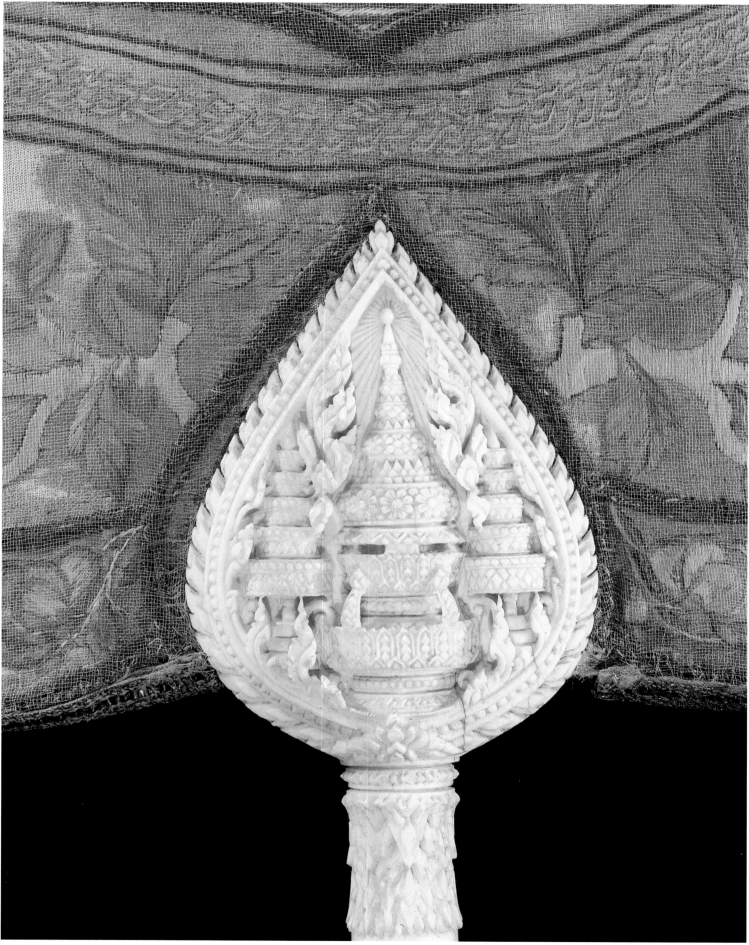

FIG 52

69

FIG 53

"**JAPANESE VASE**, embroiled with cut or engraved mother-of-pearl shells smoothly made by Siamese manufacturers."
PEARL INLAID bowl for presenting offerings and gifts
"ตลุ่มประดับมุก"
Ta lum phra dhap muk
Gift of King Mongkut, 1856
Harris Treaty Gifts
Wood, lacquer, mother-of-pearl
NMNH # 48
47 cm diameter × 28 cm height

On King Mongkut's English list, he called these "Japanese" vases. Indeed, lacquer with pearl inlay was a popular Asian art form, and King Mongkut undoubtedly knew that Americans were most familiar with East Asian arts. In fact "Japanned" was a synonym at one time for lacquer.

BUDDHIST ARTS

Mother-of-Pearl Inlaid Lacquer

Mother-of-pearl inlaid into lacquerware is a technique that is used all across Asia, but Japan is probably most famous for this technique. In Thailand, mother-of-pearl inlay lacquer is in fact closer to the Indian vessel shapes and design motifs than to the East Asian. The examples of *ta lum* offering bowls given by King Mongkut, Pra Pin Klao, and King Chulalongkorn bore exclusively floral and leafy motifs. These faceted bowls and the manuscript box, a gift of King Chulalongkorn, had straight lines and darts as division markers in the facets. The source for Mother-of-pearl in these pieces are the *Turbo* and *Trochus* snail shells found in the Gulf of Thailand. These shells are exceptionally luminescent and prized for this purpose. The combination of the time-intensive lacquer process, where a vessel is built with successive rings of split bamboo and then lacquered in a great number of layers, and the tremendous effort of designing, cutting, and placing of the tiny mother-of-pearl inlay pieces, makes this a highly prized art form normally one reserved for temple arts, court arts, and exceptional private commissions.

South and East Asian mother-of-pearl inlay technique was transformed into an entirely Thai form and lacquerware design, for objects associated with Buddhism and giftgiving as well as luxury items such as furniture, screens, and decorative storage containers. The most famous Thai inlays are elaborate temple doors and boxes and cabinets for holding religious texts. The *ta lum muk* decorated with mother-of-pearl inlay, was used to present offerings in the temple and also to hold gifts of textiles for a bride. These pearl-inlaid pieces were an essential part of a *kru'angyot* gift, and contributed to two other gift giving systems, the Buddhist merit making *tam bun* system for the maintenence of the monkhood, and the bridewealth system.[77]

FIG 54

SET OF THREE MOTHER-OF-PEARL INLAID PRESENTATION BOWLS
"ตะลุมมุกๆอเถา"
Ta lum muk nu'ng tao
Gift of King Chulalongkorn, 1876
Siam Exhibit, Centennial Exposition
Wood, lacquer, mother-of-pearl
NMNH # 27124
Large: 38 cm diameter × 22.5 cm height
Medium: 34 cm diameter × 11 cm height
Small: 27 cm diameter × 18.5 cm height

---

[77] Frazer-Lu and Krug 1982

FIG 55

**MOTHER-OF-PEARL INLAID
PRESENTATION BOWL**
"ตะลุ่มมุก"
Ta lum muk
Gift of King Chulalongkorn, 1876
Siam Exhibit, Centennial Exposition
Wood, lacquer, mother-of-pearl
NMNH # 27124b
34.3 cm diameter × 21.6 cm height

**TIERED MOTHER-OF-PEARL INLAID
PRESENTATION BOWL**
"ภานแว่นฟ้ามุก"(พาน)
Phan wan fa muk
Used for presentation of textiles
Gift of King Chulalongkorn, 1876
Siam Exhibit, Centennial Exposition
Wood, lacquer, mother-of-pearl
NMNH # 27122
20 cm diameter × 24.5 cm height

FIG 56

FIG 57

MOTHER-OF-PEARL INLAID BETEL BOX
"หีบหมากมุก"
Hip mak muk
Gift of King Chulalongkorn, 1876
Siam Exhibit, Centennial Exposition
Wood, lacquer, mother-of-pearl
NMNH # 27121
24.2 cm length × 15.5 cm depth × 10 cm
height

**DETAIL, MOTHER-OF-PEARL INLAID
BETEL BOX**
"หีบหมากมุก"
Hip mak muk
Gift of King Chulalongkorn, 1876
Siam Exhibit, Centennial Exposition
Wood, lacquer, mother-of-pearl
NMNH # 27121

FIG 58

73

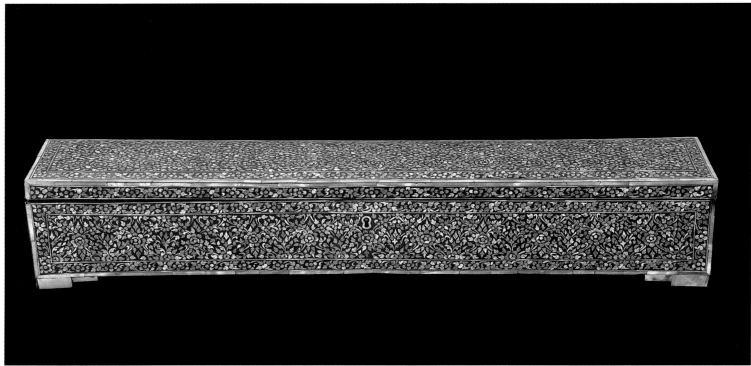

FIG 59

MOTHER-OF-PEARL INLAID BOX FOR STORING BUDDHIST DOCTRINAL MANUSCRIPTS
"ทีบใส่คำภีร์"(คัมภีร์)
Hip sai kham phi
Gift of King Chulalongkorn, 1876
Siam Exhibit, Centennial Exposition
Wood, lacquer, mother-of-pearl
NMNH # 27123
62.5 cm length × 10 cm width × 11.5 cm height

MONK'S ALMS BOWL, LID WITH EMBLEM OF STATE, AND STAND
"บาท"(บาตร)
Bat
Gift of King Chulalongkorn, 1876
Siam Exhibit, Centennial Exposition
Wood, lacquer, mother-of-pearl
USNM #s 27266
30 cm total height

This alms bowl cover is one of a series made for superior monks to mark the occasion of the second coronation ceremony of King Rama V. The design is made up of flame elements that take advantage of the natural shimmer of the *Hoy* mother-of pearl. The cover depicts the Emblem of State of Thailand, and here the *Ma-ha Wichian Mani* diamond in the pinnacle of the Great Crown of Victory emanates rays of light, the ribbon of text at the top displays King Chulalongkorn's extensive title, and at the bottom is written the day and year of his coronation. The Brahman heaven populated with thirty-three gods circles the rim of the lid, depicting *Pra In*, Indra, the Lord of Heaven with a royal procession and an audience with musical entertainment. The *rong* (stand) shows the many vehicles of gods and kings.

FIG 60

74

FIG 61

DETAIL, MONK'S ALMS BOWL WITH LID WITH EMBLEM OF STATE
"บาท"(บาตร)
Bat
Gift of King Chulalongkorn, 1876
Siam Exhibit, Centennial Exposition
Wood, lacquer and mother-of-pearl
USNM # 27266
7 cm height × 26.5 cm diameter

FIG 62

MONK'S BAG, *YAM*, WITH ALMS BOWL, COVER WITH EMBLEM OF STATE, AND STAND
"ย่าม"(ย่ามบาตร)
Gift of King Chulalongkorn, 1876
Siam Exhibit, Centennial Exposition
USNM #s 27266, 27270
Monk's bag, *yam*, 61 cm height of body (48 cm length of strap) × 84 cm diameter of opening

A monk's bowl requires a proper bag in which to carry it. This *yam*, made of imported Indian brocade, was given to the United States by King Chualalongkorn with the fan and the monk's bowl and lid following the 1876 Centennial Exposition. The *yam* is worn over the shoulder with the lidded monk's bowl inside. A monk uses a bowl such as this to accept food offerings. After accepting the offerings, the lid is replaced and the flaps of the *yam* are crossed over the bowl.

75

FIG 63

ENAMEL BETEL SET

Betel sets for monks were of copper often decorated with floral patterns and with yellow enamel, considered a suitable color and material for monks, whose yellow robes are symbols of their vow of poverty. This set was made in China for export to Siam in 1868. An inscription in Chinese on the bottom of the betel box reads: "Made at the Super-Fine Factory in the 7th Year of Tung Chi [1868]."

YELLOW ENAMEL MONK'S BETEL SET ▲
"เครื่องหมากถมปัด"
Khru'ang mak thom pat
Copper and enamel
Chinese for Thai market
Gift of King Chulalongkorn, 1876
Centennial Exposition, Siam Exhibit
USNM # 27271-4 (6 pieces)

FIG 66

76

◄◄ FROM LEFT TO RIGHT:

YELLOW ENAMEL SPITTOON
See: Fig. 66, opposite page, below

SMALL ENAMEL SPITTOON
"กะโถนถมปัด"
Ka thon thom pat
USNM # 27271
16 cm height × 12 cm diameter

YELLOW ENAMEL WATER BOWL WITH TRAY
"ขันน้ำภานรองถมปัด"(พาน)
Khan nam phan rong thom pat
USNM # 27272
11 cm diameter × 26.5 cm height

YELLOW ENAMEL BETEL BOX
See: Fig. 65, below, right

YELLOW ENAMEL CUP
"จอก"
Chok
USNM # 27271
5 cm height × 10 cm diameter

YELLOW ENAMEL WATER POT
See: Fig. 64, right

YELLOW ENAMEL WATER POT ►
"กาน้ำถมปัด"
Ka nam thom pat
Copper and enamel
Gift of King Chulalongkorn, 1876
Centennial Exposition, Siam Exhibit
USNM # 27273
11.5 cm diameter × 14 cm height

◄ YELLOW ENAMEL SPITTOON
"กะโถนถมปัด"(กระโถน)
Ka thon thom pat
Copper and enamel
Gift of King Chulalongkorn, 1876
Centennial Exposition, Siam Exhibit
USNM # 27271
30.5 cm diameter (at lip) × 19.5 cm height

YELLOW ENAMEL BETEL BOX ►
"กล่องหมากถมปัด"
Klong mak thom pat
Copper and enamel
Gift of King Chulalongkorn, 1876
Centennial Exposition, Siam Exhibit
USNM # 27274
11.5 cm diameter × 14 cm height

FIG 64

FIG 65

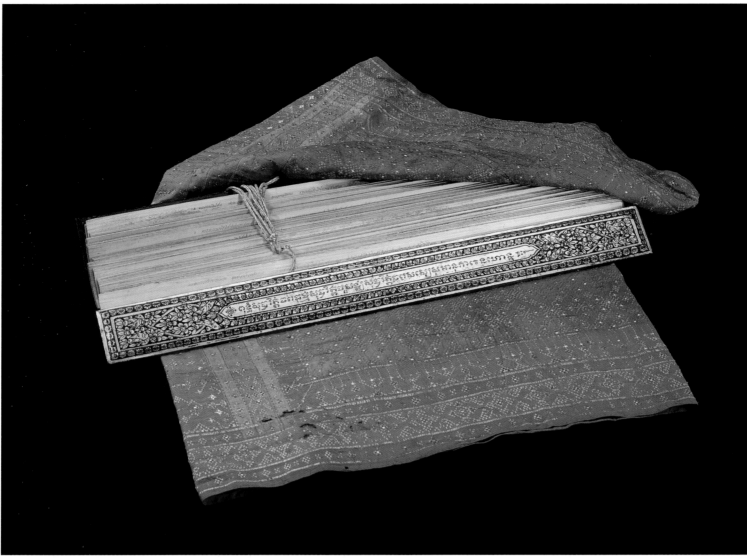

FIG 67

TRIPITAKA, OR BUDDHIST DOCTRINE
"พระไตรปิฎก"
Tripitaka
Cover is black lacquer with gold leaf design
Pages are palm leaf
Gift of State, 1949
USNM # 387077
6 cm length × 6 cm with × 9 cm thickness of text

King Mongkut's studies during his monk-hood had shown that Mon, Khmer and Sri Lankan Buddhist texts were more doctrinally pure versions than the Thai Pali versions. Therefore, many "Khmer" manuscripts such as these were actually written and used in Thailand in the nineteenth century.

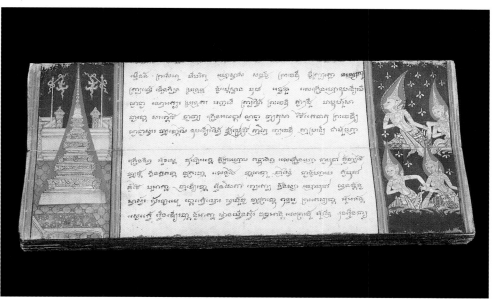

FIG 68

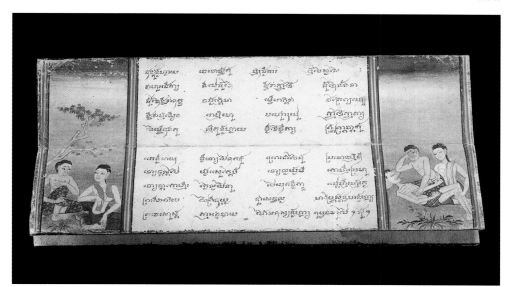

FIG 69

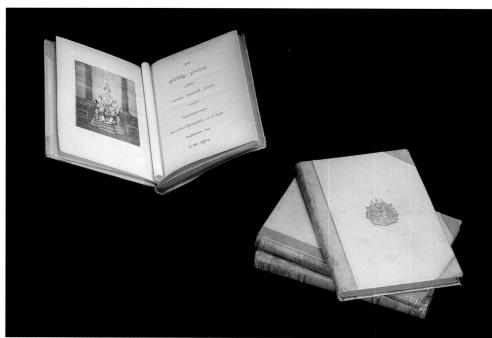

FIG 70

ILLUMINATED MANUSCRIPT OF THE
PHRA MALAI SUTRA
"พระมาลัยสูตร"
Phra Malai Sutra
Angels and a stupa
Painted *Koi* paper
Gift of State, 1966
Bicentennial of the birth of James Smithson,
founder of the Smithsonian.
USNM # 404342
66 cm length × 14 cm width

ILLUMINATED MANUSCRIPT OF THE
PHRA MALAI SUTRA
"พระมาลัยสูตร"
Preparing for a funeral
Painted *Koi* paper
Gift of State, 1966
Bicentennial of the birth of James Smithson,
founder of the Smithsonian.
USNM # 404342

The *Phra Malai Sutra* is the story of a disciple of the Buddha's, *Phra Malai*, who took a journey through the Buddhist Heavens and Hells. He took lotus buds with him as an offering to *Pra In* (Indra), Lord of Heaven. He brought back many messages from the inhabitants of Hell, who tell him to warn all of his friends and relatives to keep the Buddha's precepts and avoid a fate in Hell. In Heaven, *Phra Malai* learned of the Future Buddha and took this message of hope in the Buddha's return back to earth.

The Phra Malai Sutra is used as a source of sermons and rituals for the *Sop*, or Buddhist funerary ceremonies.

KING CHULALONGKORN'S 1893 VERSION OF THE *TRIPITAKA*
Gift of King Chulalongkorn, 1893
Dibner Rare Book Library Call # PK4546.A1-1893 RB SI

In 1893, in order to commemorate the twenty-fifth anniversary of King Chulalongkorn's accession to the throne the Royal Press produced this thirty-three volume Pali version of the "Three Baskets" of the Buddha's teachings, the *Tripitaka*, in Thai script. This project was started by his father, King Mongkut, in an effort to make the "Three Baskets" of the Buddha's teachings more accessible to Thai readers not versed in the esoteric Pali (Sanskrit-based) script often used for religious texts. Pali language written in Khmer script was considered the more pure form of the texts for quite some time, but Chulalongkorn's Thai edition contains changes suggested by King Mongkut's studies of older Sinhalese (Sri Lankan) texts. Sets were sent to major libraries around the world as a gift from the king.

NINETEENTH-CENTURY MANUSCRIPT CABINET from Wat Rakhang Khosittaram, Thonburi

"ตู้พระไตรปิฎก"

Tu Phra Traipidok

Gift of State, 1966
Bicentennial of the birth of James Smithson, founder of the Smithsonian Institution
USNM # 404341

Wood, lacquer, and gold leaf
169.5 cm height × 97 cm width × 676.5 cm depth

Scenes from the Jataka Tales, stories of the ten lives of the Buddha prior to his ultimate life as Prince Siddhartha Gautama, cover the sides of this magnificent cabinet.[78] The doors present the culmination of this theme by displaying four scenes from Siddhartha Gautama's life, leading to his adoption of the path of the ascetic searching for the Way. A dedicatory inscription on the back states the cabinet was made at Wat Rakhang Khosittaram in Thonburi. The cabinet's execution and the type of hinges used place the cabinet in the Early to Middle Bangkok Periods, 1782-1873.

Painting in gold-leaf on lacquer requires execution of the design in reverse using a water-soluble gluey mixture on the still tacky black lacquer surface. Extremely thin sheets of gold leaf are then applied to the entire side of the cabinet and the surface of lacquer and glue is allowed to dry. When fully dry, the surface of the cabinet is washed with water. Gold leaf adhering to the water-soluble glue washes away, leaving only the positive design in gold leaf firmly adhering to the dry black lacquer. Since the gold leaf is quite thin, repeated use and even exposure to sunlight quickly wears away parts of the design. While much wear is evident on this cabinet, the delicately executed design continues to shine.

FIG 71

DOORS: THE LIFE OF SIDDHARTHA GAUTAMA:

The composition on the doors proceeds counter-clockwise from lower to upper left. These depictions place two worldly events of the life of Siddhartha Gautama in the lower register, while two scenes depicting his adoption of the life of an ascetic and initiating the search for Enlightenment are above.

Lower left: Standing and grasping the branch of a *sal* tree with her right hand, Queen Mahamaya gives birth to Prince Siddhartha as two attendants kneel before her. The gods Indra (upper left) and Brahma (upper right, holding the precious infant) welcome him.

[78] Wray, Rosenfield, and Bailey 1979; Wright 1979.

FIG 75

FIG 74

FIG 72

FIG 73

Lower right: The Great Renunciation: Prince Siddhartha renounces his family. His wife and child lie sleeping at his feet while palace attendants and musicians sleep below.

Upper right: The Great Departure: Celestial beings transport Prince Siddhartha across the Anoma River, escorted by his horseman to the rear. Mara stands to his front, attempting to block his progress.

Upper left: The Ordination of Siddhartha: Prince Siddhartha cuts his hair and vows to begin life as an ascetic in search of the Way. Indra bears witnesses to the event. Brahma (with three heads) offers him an alms bowl and monks' robes. The horse who bore him and the horseman who escorted him across the Anoma River lie at his feet.

81

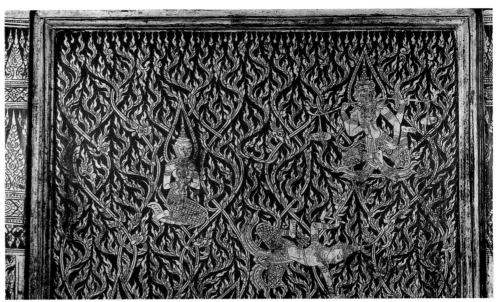
FIG 77

FIG 76

FIG 78

FIG 79

Side panels: The Jataka Tales:[79] The ten previous lives of the Buddha are important because each brings to mind an important precept that the Buddha-to-be practiced in that life. The title of the story is followed by the precept it illustrates, the specific illustration from the story depicted on the panel, and the number of that story in the listing of Jataka Tales. The Vessantara Jataka presents the penultimate life of the Buddha.

RIGHT SIDE PANEL, FULL VIEW

From top to bottom:

Top: Mahosadha Jataka (Wisdom): Kevatta kneels to retrieve Mahoda's Jewel (5).

Middle: Narada Jataka (Equanimity): Narada descends from heaven (8).

Right: Kanda-Kumara Jataka (Forbearance): Sakka breaks the sacrificial umbrella (7).

Left: Vessantara Jataka (Charity): Vessantara and his wife and children walk into the forest after giving away their chariot and horses (10).

Middle left: Temiya Jataka (Renunciation): Temiya tests his strength while Sunanda witnesses (1).

Lower left: Bhurdidatta Jataka (Moral Practice): Alambayana captures Bhurditta, the Naga Prince (6).

Lower right: Mahajanaka Jataka (Perseverence): Sivali, Mahajanaka's Queen, becomes an ascetic (2).

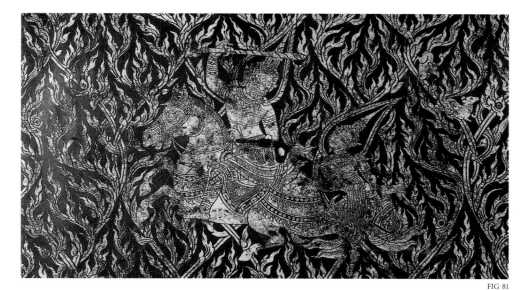

FIG 81

FIG 82

FIG 83

FIG 80

LEFT SIDE PANEL, FULL VIEW
From top to bottom:
Top: Vidhura Pandita Jataka (Truth): Vidhura hangs on to the tail of Punaka's horse (9).

Middle: Sama Jataka (Loving Kindness): King Piliyakka shoots Sama (3).

Below: Nimi Jataka (Resolution): Nimi and his escort prepare to descend to hells, while angels float in heaven above.

[79] Wray, Rosenfield, and Bailey 1979 present summary retellings of these ten Jataka Tales with illustrations from Thai temple murals. See also Wright 1979.

FIG 85

▲ JAPANESE-STYLE SAMURAI SWORD OF DAMASCUS STEEL

"The sword or dagger made of mixed steels of different colours, with its case and handle made of kew wood mounted on silver richly gilt."[80]

"ดาบเหล็กลายทำอย่างดาบยิปุ่น
ฝักไม้แก้วเครื่องเงินกาไหล่ทอง"(ดาบเหล็กลายทำอย่างญี่ปุ่น)

Dap lek lai tham yang dap Yipun
fak mai kæw khru'ang ngœn ka lai thong
Gift of King Mongkut, 1856
Harris Treaty Gifts
Pamor steel, wood, and silver
USNM # 101
87.5 cm length

This type of sword is quite unusual, a uniquely Thai interpretation of a Japanese samurai sword, with its gentle curve and "ray skin" pattern and wrapping on the hilt. The blade, certainly among the longest examples of Indonesian *pamor* metalwork, was made in Siam, though by what nationality of artisans is unknown.

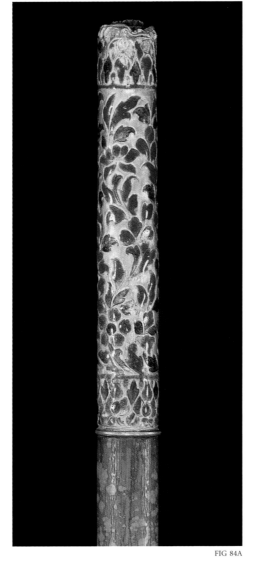

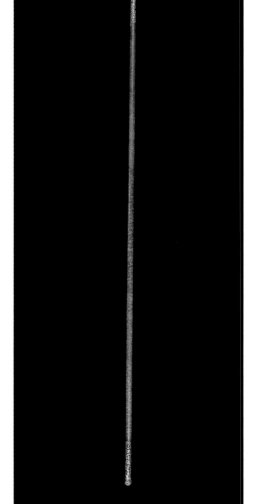

---

[80] This is King Mongkut's own English description (U.S. National Archives, Ceremonial Letters, 1856).

FIG 84A

FIG 84B

84

4. WEAPONS

Weapons were an important part of a Royal Gift, implying the mutual aid shared by allies. The sets of weapons given by King Mongkut to the United States in 1856 and in 1861 are an embodiment of the power amassed by the Thai court. Many Asian courts had long exchanged troops of ceremonial guards and artisans skilled at making weapons, and these artisans worked together to produce hybrids of Asian weapons, that combined the most auspicious features of each type. The weapons given as gifts were not commissioned especially for the president, they are items used at the court, and some seem to have been pullled directly from the palace armory.

The spotted bamboo staff decorated with gold may be a *mai phlong*, or ceremonial weapon endowed with magical protective powers like those of the Indonesian *Kris*.

The *Kris* is southern Thai or Malay in style, but the blade, of wavy damascened iron, also reflects the *pamor* craftsmanship of the Javanese court. Krises and spears were often acquired as tribute, but there is evidence that at least in the Ayutthaya period that there were Makassarese and Japanese metalworkers in the palace as well (U.S. National Archives, Ceremonial Letters). The *kris* became so important a symbol of the power of the king over the southern peninsular provinces that in the 1870s when it came time for the Thais to design a Western-style heraldic royal seal, a pair of krises assumed a prominent place on the seal along with the two important Thai symbols, Erawan and the *singha* (mythical lion).[81]

The sword is the most unusual hybrid of all. The shape and hilt are Japanese samurai style, and the blade is of Japanese shape, again of meteoric damascened iron; yet this is perhaps among the largest examples of Indonesian style damascene *pamor*. The simple and elegant sheath is of *kæw*[82] wood, native to Thailand's rain forests. King Mongkut sent President James Buchanan a similar sword in 1861, and described it as "A sword manufactured in Siam after the Japanese model with a Scabbard of Silver plated inlaid with gold & its appendages of gold . . ." This sword is kept at the United States National Archives.

The two pairs of spears pictured were of the type used by Royal Guards and often displayed in arrangements on the walls of the palace as symbols of the king's military might in fact, portraits of Thai kings are often flanked by arrangements of spears of this type (see portrait of King Chulalongkorn from the Louisiana Purchase Exposition, in the introduction).

◄ "A SIAMESE SPEAR IN BAMBOO-CANE ORNAMENTED WITH GOLD.[83]"
"ทอกค้ำไม้ไผ่เครื่องคร่ำทอง"(ไม้ไผ่)
Hok kam mai phai khru'ang khram thong
Staff (probably *Mai phlong*)
Bamboo, gold and enamel
Gift of King Mongkut, 1856
Harris Treaty Gifts
USNM # 3993
91 cm length × 1.5 cm width

This spotted-bamboo staff is probably a small symbolic weapon of the type called *mai phlong*,[84] although it is called *hok*, or spear, in King Mongkut's list and is richly decorated with gold and red and green enamel–a decorative style normally reserved for the Queen and for *Chao Fa*, celestial prince or princess rank (daughters or sons of a major queen). Most of the Thai Royal Gifts are of a noble rank and are of gold-plated silver decorated with black niello.

◄◄ DETAIL OF "A SIAMESE SPEAR IN BAMBOO-CANE ORNAMENTED WITH GOLD"[85]
Detail of: Fig. 84B

---

[81] Kalyanamitra 1977, p. 83-85.
[82] *Murraya exotica*, the "China box tree". McFarland 1944, p. 130.
[83] Throughout this section, English descriptions in quotes are King Mongkut's own translation. This is King Mongkut's own English de-

scription (U.S. National Archives, Ceremonial Letters, 1856).
[84] McFarland 1944, p. 572.
[85] This is King Mongkut's own English description.

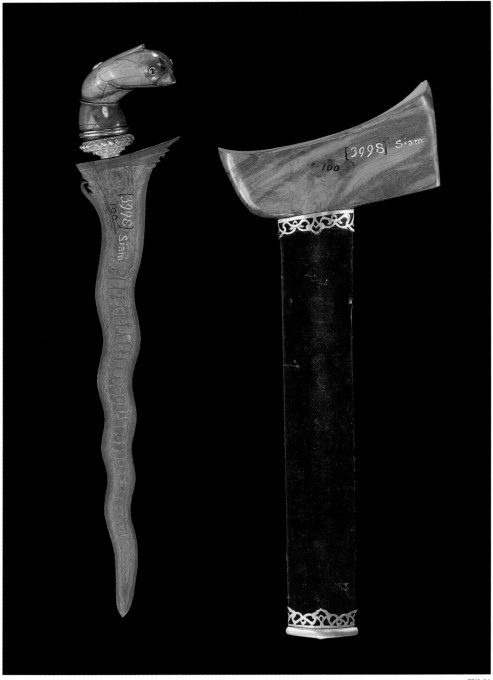

FIG 86

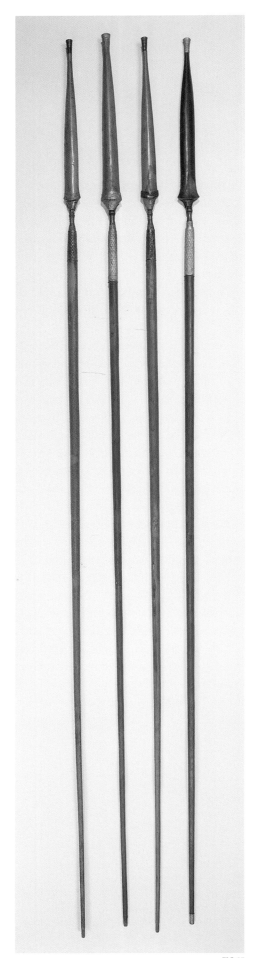

KRIS WITH AVIFORM HILT. ▲
"A finest Kris made of mixture of steels of
different colours, with its case and handle
made of kew wood ornamented with gold"[86]
"กฤษเหลกลายอย่างดีเครื่องไม้แก้วประดับด้วยทอง"
(กริชเหล็ก)
*Kris lek lai yang di khru'ang mai kæw pradap
duai thong*
Pamor steel, wood, gemstones, velvet, gold
Gift of King Mongkut, 1856
Harris Treaty Gifts
USNM # 100
44 cm length × 15 cm width at top of scabbard

---

[86] This is King Mongkut's own English description (U.S. National Archives, Ceremonial
Letters, 1856).

FIG 87

86

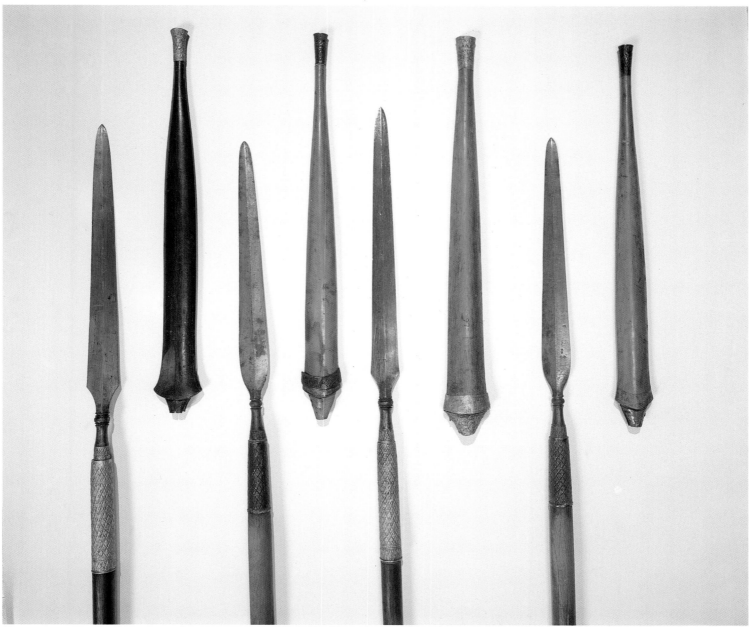

FIG 88

◄ TWO PAIRS OF SPEARS WITH
SCABBARDS
"Two pairs of spears, one pair of which were
mounted with gold, and the other with
silver"[87]
"หอกคู่เครื่องทองสอง/เครื่องเงินสอง"
Hok ku, khru'ang thong song, khru'ang ngœn
song
Wood, steel, gold, and silver
Gift of King Mongkut, 1856
Harris Treaty Gifts
USNM #s 96; 97; 98; 99
96: 200.5 cm total length, 33 cm length of
spear point
97: 203 cm total length, 35.5 cm length of
spear point
98: 205 cm total length, 41 cm length of spear
point
99: 205 cm total length, 41 cm length of spear
point

DETAIL OF SPEAR POINTS AND
SCABBARDS
Two pairs of spears with scabbards
"Two pairs of spears, one pair of which were
mounted with gold, and the other with
silver"[88]
"หอกคู่เครื่องทองสอง/เครื่องเงินสอง"
Hok ku, khru'ang thong song, khru'ang ngœn
song
Gift of King Mongkut, 1856
Harris Treaty Gifts
Wood, steel, gold, and silver
USNM #s 96; 97; 98; 99

Infantry spearbearers were an essential compo-
nent in the military guards of the king and
high-ranking princes. The guards were an important part of processions in Southeast Asian
courts.

[87] This is King Mongkut's own English description (U.S. National Archives, Ceremonial
Letters, 1856).
[88] This is King Mongkut's own English description (U.S. National Archives, Ceremonial
Letters, 1856).

FIG 89

5. TEXTILES

When the king bestowed a rank upon a person, he provided the recipient with all of the equipment necessary to perform duties in the realm of the Thai court. Gifts of textiles were essential, since they are the uniform worn during audiences with the king and since access to the imported Indian textiles and to the finest Thai and Khmer silks which made up this court uniform were highly restricted.

But because this gift is a gift to the leader of a Western nation it is far more than merely a bestowal of rank on the President. With this gift King Mongkut and "Second King" Phra Pin Klao are responding to a set of gifts sent by President Franklin Pierce, including precious scientific books for these two scientist-kings. Since the court of Siam reserved the use of fine Indian satin weaves and other textiles for court use, Phra Pin Klao emphasized the value of his gift of textiles in his inventory: "Case marked '1' contains elegant and costly specimens of Siamese garments."[90] Many of the imported textiles they sent were woven with Thai design motifs; some pieces given by Phra Pin Klao were Indian or Chinese in design, but they were made into jackets of Thai cut. One piece in particular is quite fine and seems to be an early nineteenth century piece, called by Phra Pin Klao "1 Silk Cloth, richly wrought with gold, called by us *Pha yok thong klet phum sen*"[91] (USNM # 89).

King Mongkut sent a total of six textiles to President Franklin Pierce, while Phra Pin Klao sent eleven pieces, including tailored garments. King Mongkut included an inventory of his gifts in both Thai script and in English, although his English list offers general descriptions and not a direct translation of the Thai. Phra Pin Klao's list is a very descriptive English list with romanized Thai terms.

The silk industry in Thailand is quite well developed, with a remarkable time-depth; 4,000-year-old silk fragments were discovered at Ban Chiang, an early archeological site in northeast Thailand. Thai silks are famous for the excellent quality of the silk and for their intricate *mudmee (ikat)* designs made from silk threads pre-dyed into a pattern that emerges when the threads are woven into a fabric. Growing and weaving of cotton are also important in Thailand. In addition to the traditional courtly textiles, King Chulalongkorn selected a number of textiles from rural areas of Thailand to send along to the Siam Exhibit at the 1876 Centennial Exposition.

Once again, the interpretation of the royal gifts is quite clear. As with the weapons, King Mongkut, Phra Pin Klao, and King Chulalongkorn are garnering all of the prestige available to them in the form of exotic imported and fine domestic textiles, and as with all reciprocity, communicating the value of the relationship with the gift itself in the hope that the receiver will recognize that value and implied respect in the physical objects. The language used in the lists of gifts and in Royal letters alternated between calling attention to the costliness of the items within Thailand, and the relative poorness of the gifts compared to Western goods. This is especially ironic given the artistic mastery evidenced in this set of textiles.

◄ **SILK HIP WRAPPER WITH GOLD SUPPLEMENTARY WEFT**
"ผ้ายกทอง"
Pha yok thong
Silk, natural dyes, *mudmee* ikat tie-dyed weft threads, supplementary weft gold threads
Gift of King Chulalongkorn, 1876
Centennial Exposition
USNM # 27129
370 cm length × 95 cm width

This textile has weft strings that are tie-died before weaving (called *ikat* in Indonesian and *mudmee* in Thai) which creates the borders that run the length of the piece. This type of gold supplelementary weft, or *yok thong*, seems to come from the southern city-state of Nakhorn Sri Thammarat.[89]

[89] Gittinger and Lefferts 1992, p 151.
[90] (U.S. National Archives, Ceremonial Letters, 1856).
[91] U.S. National Archives, Ceremonial Letters, 1856.

**"1 SILK CLOTH, RICHLY WROUGHT
WITH GOLD. CALLED BY US PHA YOK
THONG KLET PHUM SEN"**
"ผ้ายกทองเกล็ดปูมเส้น"
Pha yok thong klet phum sen
Gift of "Second King" Phra Pin Klao, 1856
Harris Treaty Gifts
USNM # 89
326 cm length × 96 cm width

FIG 90

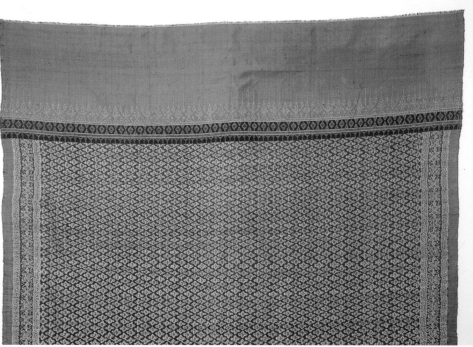

"GILT SILK CLOTH"
"ผ้ายกทอง"
Pa yok thong
Gift of King Mongkut, 1856
Harris Treaty Gifts
Silk, gold threads, natural dyes, *mudmee*
tie-dyed weft threads, supplementary weft
USNM # 79
128 cm length × 95 cm width

FIG 91

GOLD AND SILVER THREAD SUPPLEMENTARY WEFT TEXTILES

Supplementary weft decoration in the Smithsonian's Thai collection ranges from the Malay-style *Songket* seen in USNM #s 89 and 27127, to the refined band-dyed Nakhon Sri Thammarat pieces (USNM # 27129 and the textile wrapping of the Buddhist text USNM # 387077), to the less formal decorative borders seen in USNM #s 27133 and 27134. Even less formal textiles were ornamented with gold supplementary weft threads.

FIG 92

SILK HIP WRAPPER WITH GOLD SUPPLEMETARY WEFT
"ผ้ายกทอง"
Pha Yok Thong
Gift of King Chulalongkorn, 1876
Centennial Exposition
USNM # 27127
96.5 cm width × 336 cm length

CLOTH WITH SMALL, SQUARE CHECKED DESIGNS
"ผ้าตาสมุก"
Pha ta sa muk
Gift of King Chulalongkorn, 1876
Centennial Exposition
Silk, natural dyes
USNM # 27133
320 cm length x 98 cm width

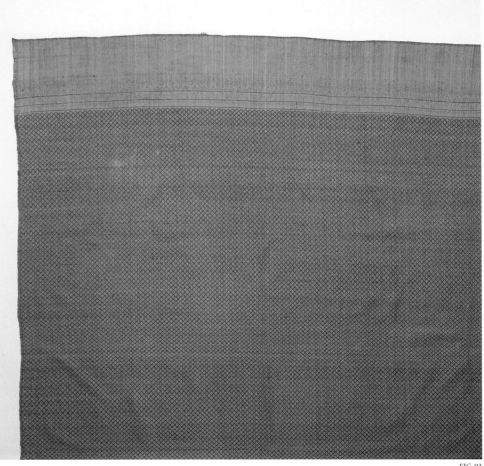

FIG 93

CLOTH WITH SESAME-SEED PATTERN
"ผ้าตาเลตงา"
Pha ta let nga
Gift of King Chulalongkorn, 1876
Centennial Exposition
USNM # 27134
317 cm length × 93.5 cm

FIG 94

The four pillows and curtains seen here are Indian brocade *khem*. These pillows and many others were included with gifts of furniture and transportation items such as palanquins and elephant howdahs.

FIG 95

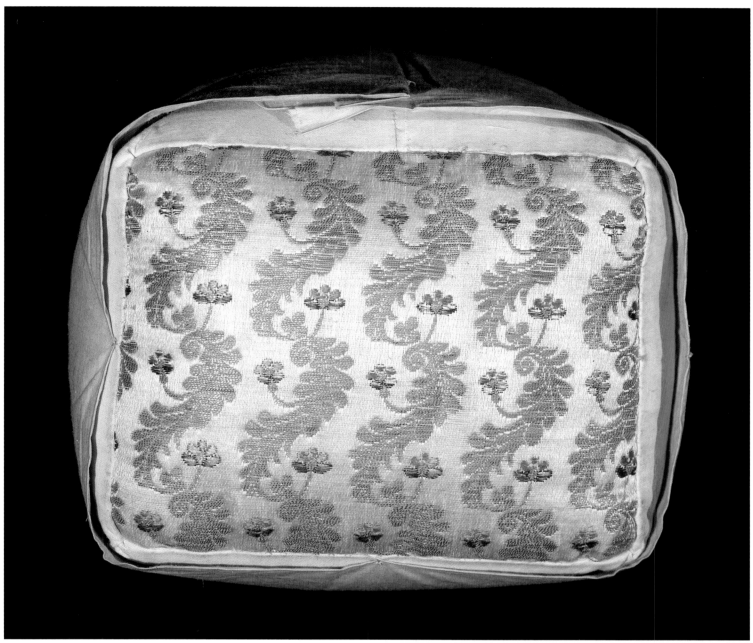

FIG 96

◄ ▲PILLOWS

**RECTANGULAR EMBROIDERED PILLOWS
FOR RECLINING**
"หมอนอิง"
Mon ing
Gift of King Chulalongkorn, 1876
Centennial Exposition, Siam Exhibit
USNM # 27281
13 cm length × 13 cm width × 15 cm depth

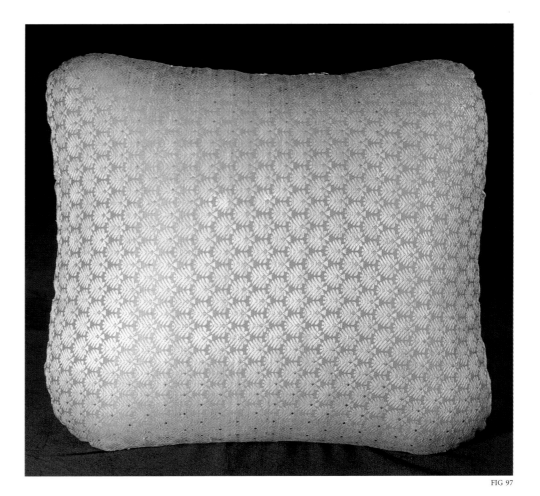

FIG 97

**PAIR OF SQUARE EMBROIDERED
PILLOWS**
"หมอนเหลี่ยมน่าปัก"
Mon liam na pak
Gift of King Chulalongkorn, 1876
Centennial Exposition, Siam Exhibit
USNM # 27141
32 cm × 32 cm

FIG 98

94

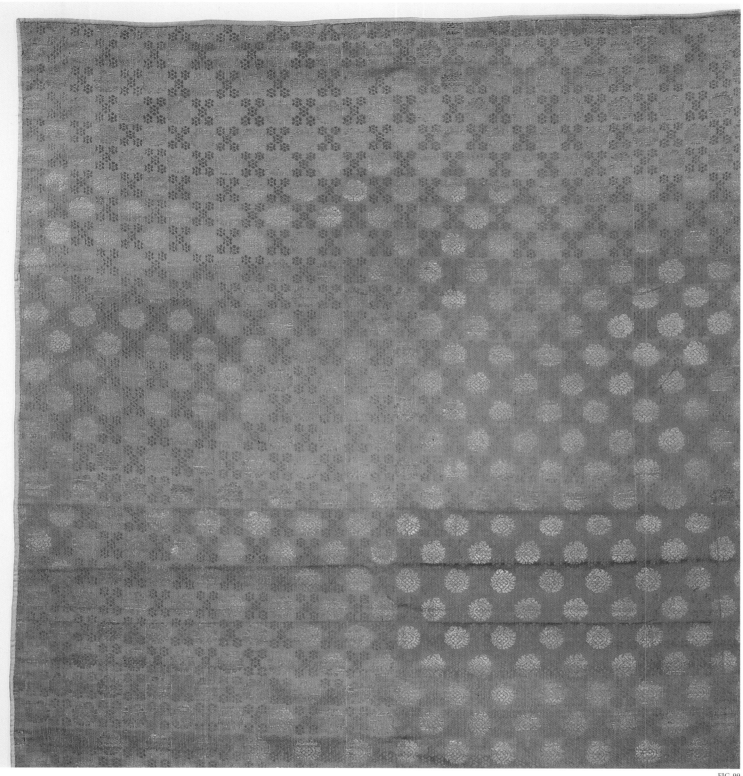

FIG 99

SILK FLOWERED CURTAIN
"ม่านผ้าไหมลายดอกไม้"
Man pha mai lai dok mai
Gift of King Chulalongkorn, 1876
Centennial Exposition, Siam Exhibit
USNM # 27142
181 cm length × 70 cm wide

FIG 100

MUDMEE SILKS

KHMER SILK
"Silk Cloth, Richly figured"
Khmer *mudmee* silk hip wrapper
With *Naga* (sacred snake) pattern
"ผ้าปูมเขมร"
Pha pum kamen
Gift of "Second King" Phra Pin Klao, 1856
Harris Treaty Gifts
USNM # 81
323 cm length × 95 cm width

THAI SILK
"Two pieces of Poom cloth of second quality"
"ผ้าปูมไทย"
Pha Pum Thai
(Thai "second quality")
Salmon colored with diamond pattern
Gift of King Mongkut, 1856
Harris Treaty Gifts
Silk, natural dyes, weft *mudmee*
USNM # 83a
318 cm length × 96 cm width

FIG 101

FIG 102

THAI SILK
Pha Pum Thai
"ผ้าปูมไทย"
(Thai "second quality")
Silk, natural dyes, weft *mudmee (ikat)*
Gift of King Mongkut, 1856
Harris Treaty Gifts
USNM # 83 b
326 cm length × 94 cm width

King Mongkut may have called these pieces "second quality" because of the rather thick grade of silk, which is not as fine as the Khmer silks in the Smithsonian's Thai collection (such as USNM # 81, above), and because the tie dyed *mudmee* weft pattern did not quite match up. However, the rich red, purple, burgundy, green, gold, and blue dyes are certainly very good quality.

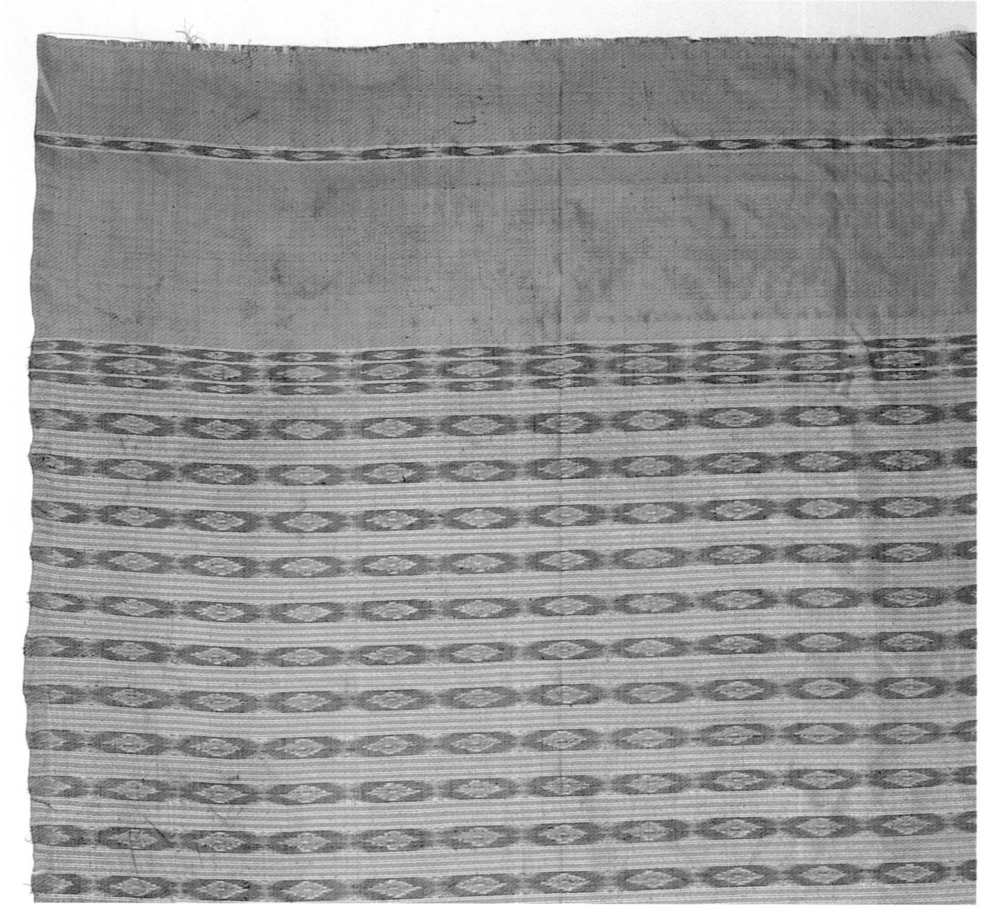

SILK HIP WRAPPER
"ยกไหมน่าเกบ"
Yok mai nah kep
Mudmee tie-dyed weft, natural dyes
Gift of King Chulalongkorn, 1876
Centennial Exposition
USNM # 27126
335.28 cm length × 98 cm width

FIG 103

GARMENTS

Finished garments were another category of textile gift included in the insignia set. In some cases, the textiles were imported Indian, Chinese or Japanese fabrics, but the cut of the garments is unmistakenly Thai.

"1 COAT. *SUA KHEM KHAP YANG NOI*"
"เสื้อเขมกับ"(เสื้อเข้มขาบ)
Sua khem khap yang noi
Gift of "Second King" Phra Pin Klao, 1856
Harris Treaty Gifts
USNM # 86
74 cm length × width 50.5 cm

This Indian brocade *khem* is sewn into a Thai coat pattern with flaring hem. With the influx of Westerners in the late 1850s some of whom were often present at court, King Mongkut declared that jackets must be worn by all Thai princes and noblemen during Royal Audiences.

"1 JACKET, PLAIN. WITH FIVE GOLD BUTTONS. SUA SAN PHRAE"
"เสื้อส้นแพร"
Sua san phrae
Gift of "Second King" Phra Pin Klao, 1856
Harris Treaty Gifts
USNM # 88
48 cm × 60.5 cm (total width at sleeve)

DETAIL OF BUTTONS
"1 Jacket, plain. *Sua san phrae*"
"เสื้อส้นแพร"
Sua san phre
Gift of "Second King" Phra Pin Klao, 1856
Harris Treaty Gifts
USNM # 88

This light blue man's jacket has a Chinese pattern twill weave and exquisite gold cloisoné buttons.

FIG 106

FIG 104

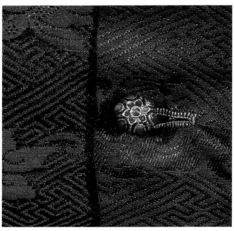

FIG 105

FIG 107

CHIENG MAI THAI SARONG.
Probably from court of Chieng Mai.[92]
Cotton, silk, and gold thread
Gift of King Chulalongkorn, 1876
Siam Exhibit, Centennial Exposition
USNM # 27282
134 cm length × 68 cm width

---

[92] Fraser-Lu 1988, pp. 105-118. The three-piece design with the central striped body and the richly woven border piece or *thinjok* indicates that this was made for a high-ranking woman in a northern Thai court.

FIG 108

GOLD LACE NOBLEMAN'S ROBE

"ฉลองพระองค์ครุย"

Chalong Phra Ong Khrui
Silk, gold, and platinum or white gold
Gift of Prince Wan Waitayakon, 1947
USNM # 385867
98 cm length × 79 cm width

Family tradition has it that this fine nineteenth-century gold lace robe, *Chalong Phra Ong Khrui*, covered with the flame motif belonged originally to King Mongkut when he was a young prince. Prince Naradhip, son of King Mongkut, who was born in 1861, is often pictured wearing the robe, which he passed along to his son, Prince Wan Waithayakorn, who became ambassador to the United States and donated the robe to the Smithsonian in 1947. Prince Wan went on to become the president of the General Assembly of the United Nations. This type of robe forms part of a *khru'ang yot*, or insignia set of a nobleman. It was worn on state occasions but has now been replaced, for the most part, by business suits, Western-style military uniforms, and tuxedos.

Khrui, gold lacework, was made for centuries in the Thai court for the use of kings, Queens, *Choa Fa* (H.R.H. Rank Celestial Princes and Princesses) and *Phra Ong Chao* (children of consorts of the King). This robe probably dates from at least as early as the Fourth Reign (1851-1868) because, beginning in the Fifth Reign (1868-1910) such robes were often encrusted with newly-created lace and embroidery renderings of orders or insignia instituted in the late Fourth and Fifth Reigns.

6. ROYAL TRANSPORTATION

King Chulalongkorn sent a fleet of model Royal Barges as part of the Siam exhibit to be displayed at the 1876 Centennial Exposition in Philadelphia. This gift underscored the grandeur of Royal life during the Reign of King Rama V, and they can clearly be seen prominently displayed in contemporary photographs of the exposition (see introduction). Because of this gift, and the vagaries of history, the United States owns models of barges which no longer exist. The prime example of this is the model of the special escort *Akchai* barge *Rua Sri Samat Chai*. While many old photographs of this barge exist, the Smithsonian model remains perhaps the most nearly complete record of this exquisite Ayutthaya-period filigree and bejeweled masterpiece.[93]

Thai Kings and nobles have moved through the landscape on a number of important vehicles, ranging from palanquins to elephants, barges, and chariots. Prior to King Mongkut's reign (r. 1851-1868), it was believed that the Royal personage should not be permitted to touch the profane earth, lest disasters thereby occur.[94] Since King Rama IV, however, many such restrictions on Their Majesties' public lifes have been lifted.

At the Coronation Ceremony, the Chief Court Brahmin recites various Vedic incantations to open the gates of Heaven whereby the Trinity of Hindu Gods descend into the person of the King. In Thai eyes today, the King does not become divine, or a god, but rather a *Somuthi Thep*, "an imaginary god." As an imaginary god, His Majesty participates in the aura of Shiva, Vishnu, and Bhrama and thus must use their conveyances when performing his duties. Shiva is primarily seen as moving over land. Since Shiva rides Nandi, the Bull, His Majesty as Shiva is borne on a palanquin by members of the Royal Household who act as his vehicle. When His Majesty walks on the ground, he walks on a carpet of red or another color. Shiva's feet are not permitted to touch the ground since, for example, when he does the cosmic dance as *Shiva Nataraj*, a holocaust would occur and the end of the world would be forthcoming.

His Majesty is seen as possessing characteristics of Vishnu when he travels at a speed faster than a walk. Thus, travelling by car, plane, helicopter, or train requires the display of the yellow Royal Standard with red Garuda, Vishnu's mount. When Vishnu the protector walks the earth he does so in the guise of Rama who is the human King who can go wherever he wants.

When His Majesty travels across water, he does so as the god Brahma and is borne on his mount, the *hamsa* swan, *Suphannahongse* barge, by riverine procession.

From at least the time of Ayutthaya to the present, the royal barges have been used in royal ceremonies such as the *Kathin Luang*, when the King travels by water to present robes to monks resident in Royal monasteries in October at the end of the Rains Retreat. For this procession, the robes to be presented are placed on the *Anandanakkarat* barge, with a prow ornament in the shape of a mythical multi-headed *Naga* serpent.

The third Royal barge is the *Anekajatibhujonga*. This barge is used to carry the King's immediate family in Royal procession.

These three barges travelled in the core of the flotilla, surrounded by barges with other functions. Wherever the King travelled, whether on land or water, he was preceded by drummers who heralded his approach. In processions that included

[93] Dhammadhibet n.d., p. 33.
[94] Wales 1931

dozens, sometimes hundreds, of barges, the crews performed rhythmic chants and recited songs in an unceasing hymn of praise for the King, his barges, and the natural beauty of Thailand. *Samatchai,* crocodile barges, followed drum boats in the lead of the procession. Barges depicting and carrying the names of characters from the Thai literary epic, the *Ramakien,* call forth the hero, Rama's, guardian forces of magical monkeys and birds.[95] Finally, outer flanking barges, *Dang,* are simple yet elegant craft equipped with yak-hair garlands for protection.[96]

In the past, in addition to conveying the King in Royal Processions, these barges were used in splendid processions to transport letters and gifts from Heads of State to the Grand Palace, since the written word of such a personage was considered an integral part of that person. These processions astounded visitors to the Bangkok court and descriptions of them fill many pages of their letters and dispatches home. The following depiction of some of the barges from the Smithsonian collection groups them in order of a barge procession.

The following poetic description of the sights and sounds of a Royal barge procession was written by Prince Dhammadhibet (1715?-1755), eldest son of King Boromkot of Ayutthaya:

> *In Praise of the Barges*
> Verses for the Royal Barge Procession
> *by* Prince Dhammadhihibet[97]
>
> When the King journeys on Water
> He graces the jeweled throne
> Amid his magnificent entourage
> Of golden barges in proud procession.
>
> The king journeys by water
> On the glorious Royal Barge
> That sparkles like jewels
> Gleaming paddles dip and rise.
>
> Barges shaped like mighty beasts
> Throng the sovereign fleet
> Attendant barges with flying banners
> Stir the turbulent tide.
>
> — — —
>
> Sonorous music swells
> Voices and drums resound
> Barge songs echo loud
> Intoned by the jubilant crews.[98]

[95] For further information on the Ramakien see Cadet 1970 and Diskul and Rice 1982.

[96] Davis et al 1995, pp. 19-58.

[97] Translated by Khunying Chamnongsri Rutnin, Office of the Private Secretary to Her Majesty Queen Sirikit, Chitralada Palace, Bangkok

[98] Dhammadhibet n.d., p.15.

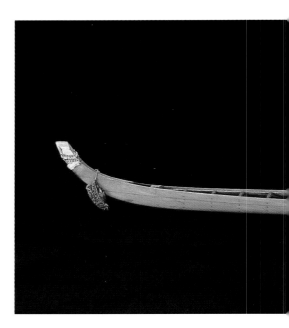

ROYAL BARGE MODELS

In the order of a Royal Barge Procession

The Royal Barge Procession is a highly choreographed event with barges arranged in a particular order depending on the occassion. In the past, it was necessary for the king's barges to be flanked by police and military barges, some with cannons mounted on the bows. The Royal Barges proper, carrying the King and Royal Family members, were protected at the core of the flotilla.

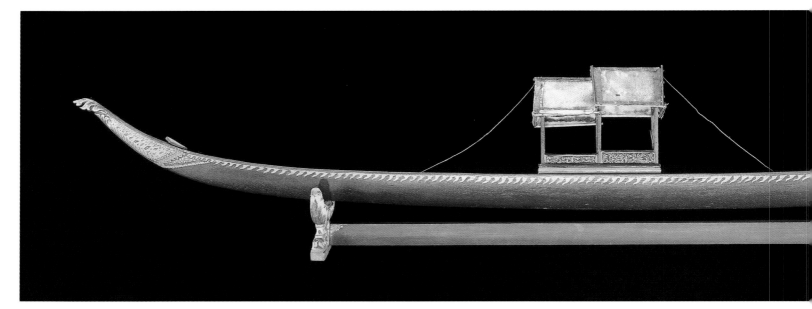

TIGER BARGES

TIGER BARGE ▲
"เรือทยานชลเสือ"(เรือเสือทะยานชล)
Su'a Thayanchon
Gift of King Chulalongkorn, 1876
Centennial Exposition, Siam Exhibit
USNM # 27326 (160266)
91.8 cm length × 7.2 cm width

TIGER BARGE ▶
Detail of prow
See: Fig. 111, above

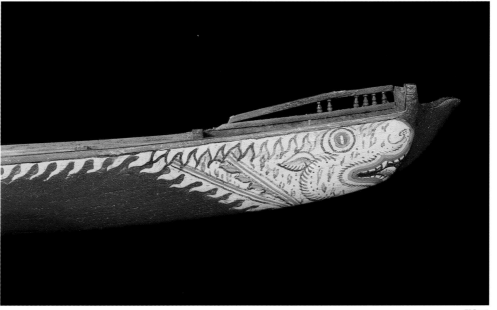

FIG 112

FIG 109

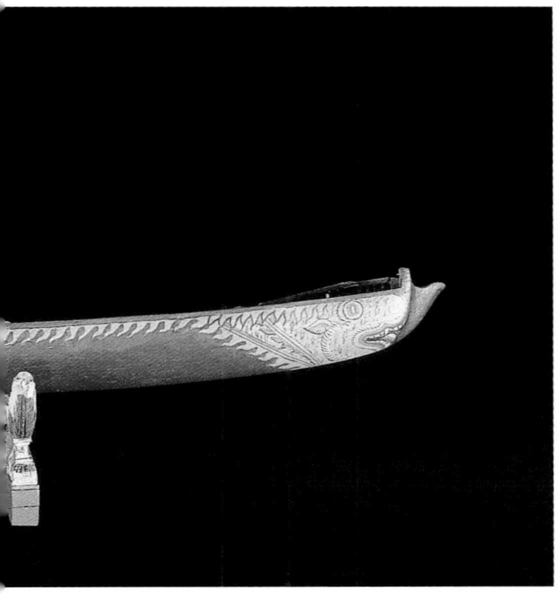

DANG ESCORT BARGES

▲ *DANG* BARGE
"เรือดั้ง"
Ru'a Dang
Gift of King Chulalongkorn, 1876
Centennial Exposition, Siam Exhibit
USNM # 160281
125 cm length × 7.7 cm width

FIG 111

◄ *DANG* BARGE
Pavilion (detail)
See: Fig. 109, above

FIG 110

103

KRABI CLASS BARGES

HANUMAN (MONKEY KING) BARGE
หนุมาน
"เรือกะบี่ปราบเมืองมาร"(เรือกระบี่ปราบเมืองมาร)
Ru'a Krabi Prab Mu'ang Marn Nat
(Hanuman)
Gift of King Chulalongkorn, 1876
Centennial Exposition, Siam Exhibit
USNM # 27332 (160282)
120 cm length × 8.3 cm width

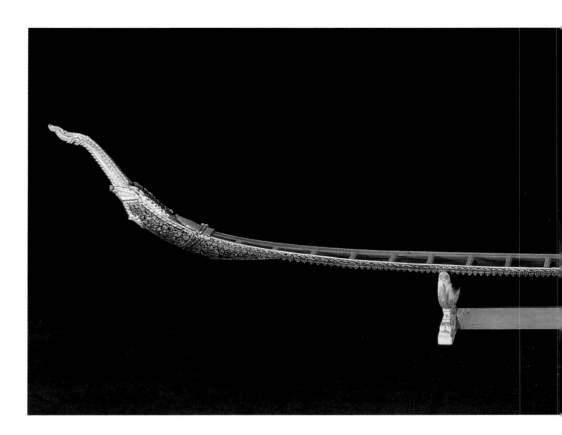

FIG 115

104

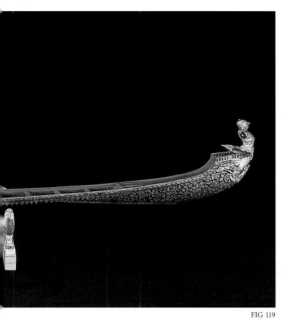

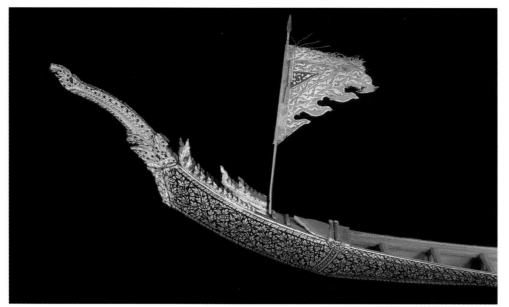

FIG 119

FIG 121

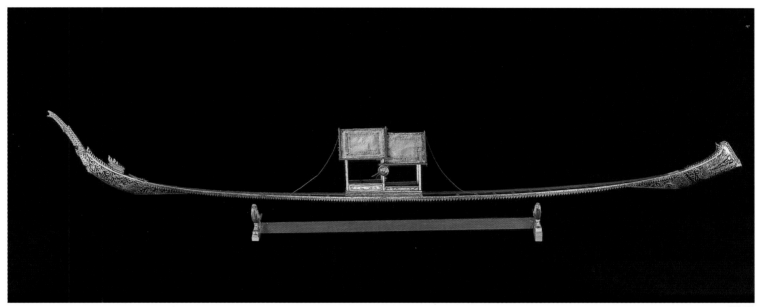

FIG 122

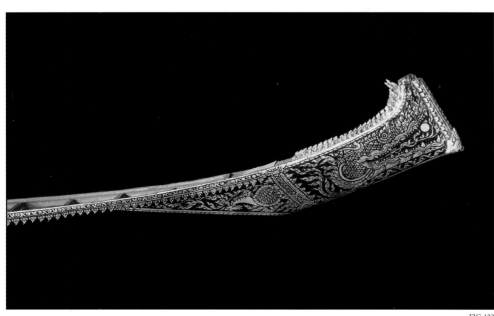

FIG 123

▲ *KHRUT*
Detail of stern with flag
See: Fig. 119, opposite page, above

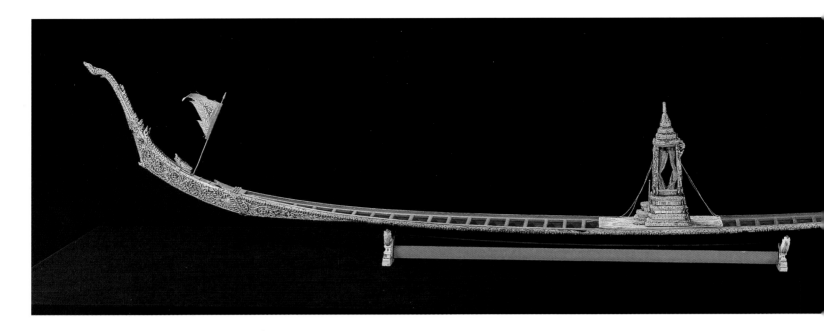

SAMAT CHAI BARGE ▲
เรือศรีสมรรถชัย
Rua Sri Samat Chai
Gift of King Chulalongkorn, 1876
Centennial Exposition, Siam Exhibit·
USNM # 160278
168 cm length × 13 cm width

SAMAT CHAI BARGE ▶
Detail of *busabuk* throne
See: Fig. 124, above

FIG 126

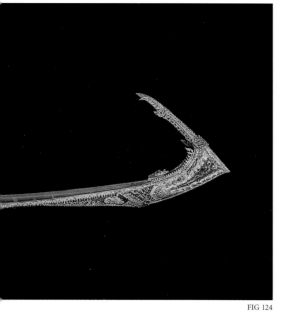

FIG 124

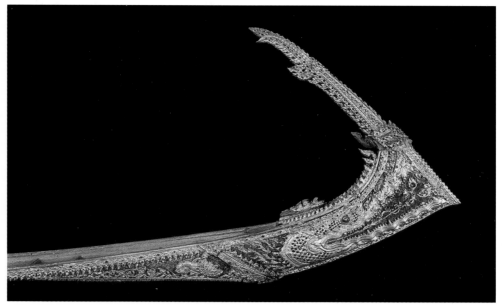

FIG 125

SAMAT CHAI BARGE ▲
Detail of prow
See: Fig. 124, above left

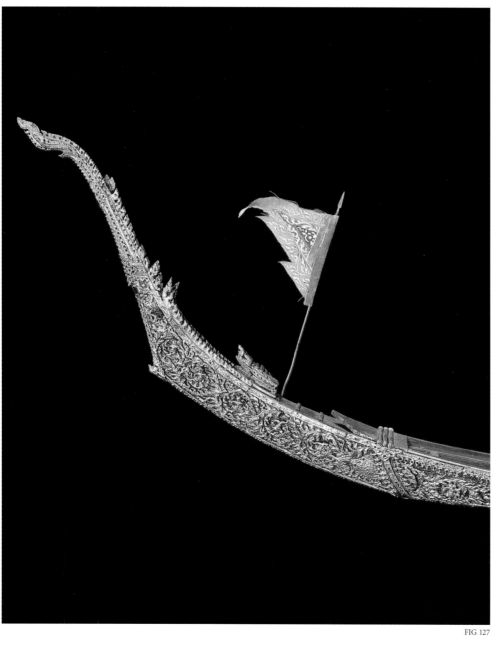

FIG 127

SAMAT CHAI BARGE
Detail of stern, with flag
See: Fig. 124, above left

ROYAL BARGES
FOR THE KING'S USE[99]

ANEKAJATIBHUJONGA ▶
เรือเอนกชาติภุชงค์
Royal Barge with yak hair and *naga* motif on prow.
Gift of King Chulalongkorn, 1876
Centennial Exposition, Siam Exhibit
USNM # 160287
160.5 cm length × 13 cm width

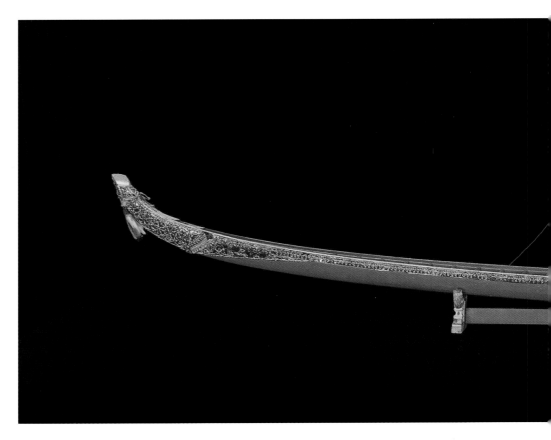

ANEKAJATIBHUJONGA ▶
Detail of prow
See: Fig. 128, above

ANEKAJATIBHUJONGA ▶▶
Pavilion (detail)
See: Fig. 128, above

[99] The Smithsonian's collection also includes models of the Royal Barges *Suphanahongse* and *Anandanakkarat*, but they are in early stages of restoration at this time.

FIG 129

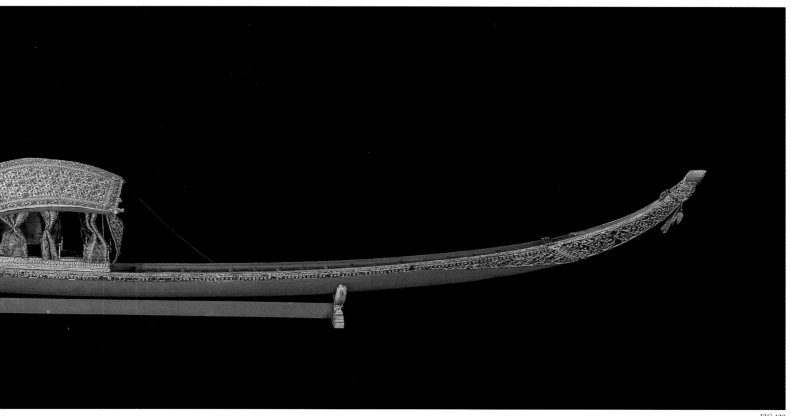

FIG 128

FIG 130

DRAGON BARGES

DRAGON BARGE
"เรือเหรา"
Ru'a Hera
Gift of King Chulalogkorn, 1876
Siam Exhibit, Centennial Exposition
USNM # 160267
106 cm length × 7.8 cm width

DRAGON BARGE ▶▶
Detail of prow
See: Fig. 131

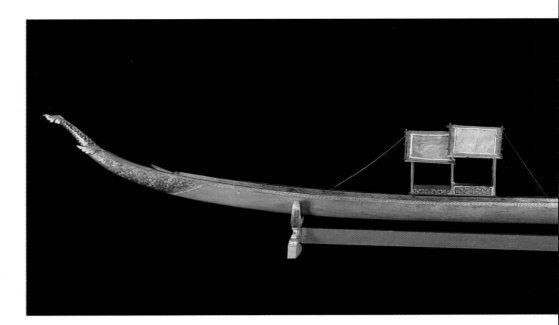

DRAGON BARGE
"เรือเหรา"
Ru'a Hera
Gift of King Chulalogkorn, 1876
Siam Exhibit, Centennial Exposition
USNM # 160275
127.5 cm length × 10 cm width

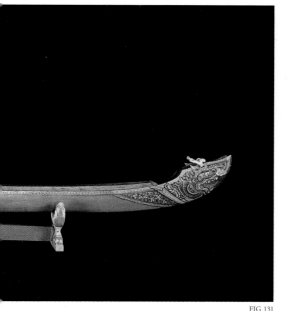

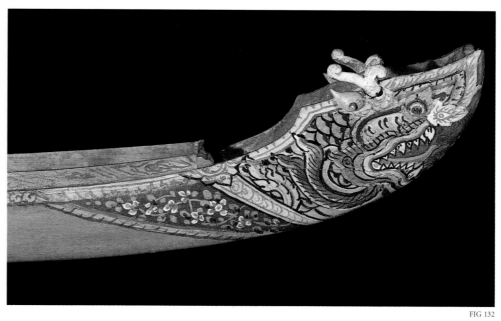

FIG 131

FIG 132

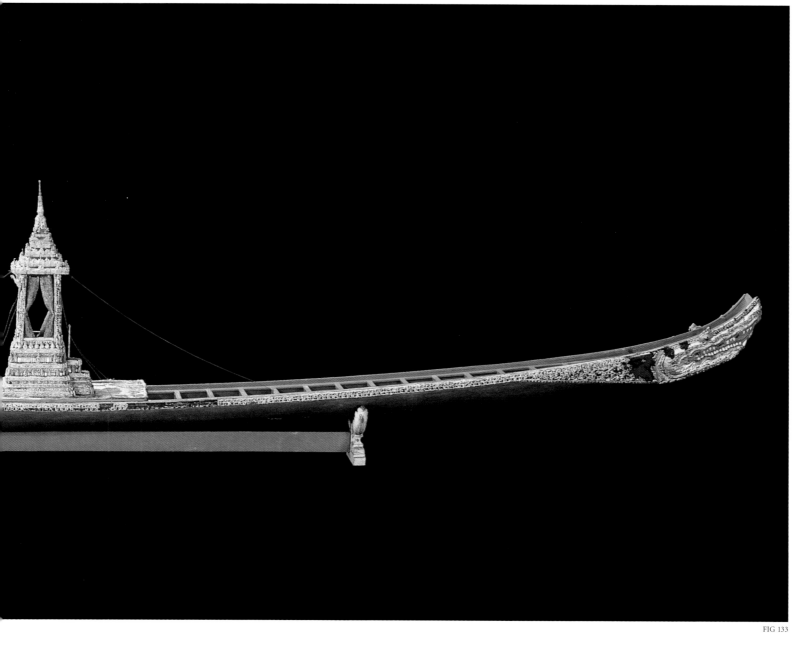

FIG 133

FIG 134

DRAGON BARGE
Detail of prow
See: Fig. 133, pp. 114-115

DRAGON BARGE ▶
Detail of *busabuk* throne
See: Fig. 133, pp. 114-115

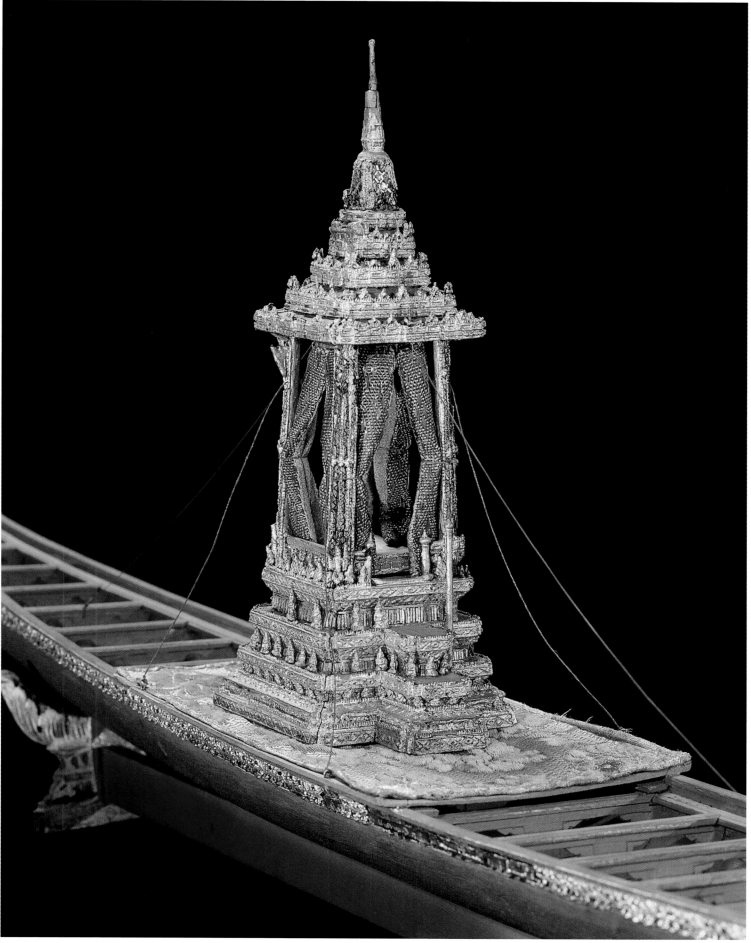

FIG 135

117

TRANSPORTATION ON LAND

FIG 136

SADDLE
"อานม้า"
An
Gift of King Chulalongkorn, 1876
Centennial Exposition, Siam Exhibit
USNA # 27204 (180166)

FIG 137

FIG 138

ELEPHANT HOWDAH
"สับประคับ"(สับคับ)
Gift of King Chulalongkorn, 1876
Siam Exhibit, Centennial Exposition
USNM # 180168
136 cm length × 77.5 cm width × 76 cm
height

PALANQUIN
"สีวิกา"
Siwika
Gift of King Chulalongkorn, 1876
Siam Exhibit, Centennial Exposition
USNM # 27259

119

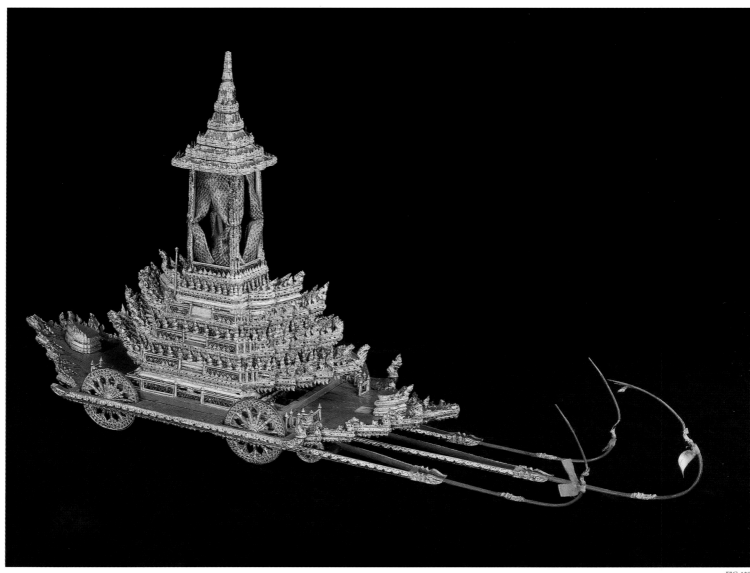

FIG 139

ROYAL FUNERAL CHARIOT ▲
"พระมหาพิไชยราชรถ"
Phra Maha Pichai Raja Rot
Gift of King Chulalongkorn, 1876
Centennial Exposition, Siam Exhibit
USNM # 27367
40.9 cm length × 21 cm width × 40 cm
height

ROYAL FUNERAL CHARIOT ▶
Detail of *busabuk* throne
See: Fig. 139, above

The *Rot* is used to transport the body of the
King and other members of the royal family to
the funeral pyre. One of a pair, the other is
called *Wejaiyan Raja Rot*.

FIG 140

121

FIG 141

CEREMONIAL INSTRUMENTS

"A GREAT SIAMESE DRUM OR TOM-TOM PEAKED WITH SILVER PEAKS"
"กลองใหญ่อย่างไทยแซ่เงิน"
Klong yai yang Thai
Gift of King Mongkut, 1856
Harris Treaty Gifts
USNM # 68 (3947)
44 cm diameter × 46.2 cm height

DRUM
"กลองชะนะ"(กลองชนะ)
Klaung Chana
Gift of King Chulalongkorn, 1876
Siam Exhibit, Centennial Exposition
USNM # 27257
47 cm diameter × 51 cm height

7. DRUMS, GONGS, AND MUSICAL INSTRUMENTS

Processions and Royal Audiences.

At court, drums and gongs were used to announce the king's presence and to herald events of all kinds They were included in Royal Gifts so that the recipient could use them on important ceremonial occasions. King Mongkut, Phra Pin Klao, and King Chulalongkorn sent several sets of ceremonial drums to the United States including "Great Siamese Drums", Malay drums, and Karen drums.

"A SET OF A PAIR OF LONG DRUMS"
A set of drums, one end "male", one "female"
"กลองผู้/กลองเมีย"
Klong phu; Klong mia
Gift of King Mongkut, 1856
Harris Treaty Gifts
USNM # 67 (3945),
73 cm height × 34 cm diameter (male),
32 cm (female)
USNM # 69 (3946)
72 cm height × 35 cm diameter (male),
32 cm (female)

FIG 142

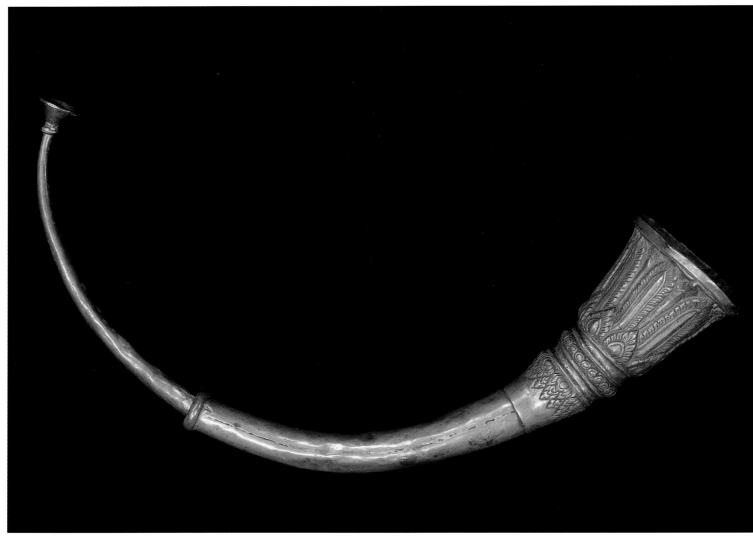

FIG 143

HORN (BUFFALO-HORN-SHAPED)
"แกรงอน"(แตรงอน)
Kra ngon
Gift of King Chulalongkorn, 1876
Siam Exhibit, Centennial Exposition
USNM # 27293
32 cm length × 8 cm diameter at mouth

"1 BRASS GONG" GONG AND MALLET
"โหม่ง"
Mong
Gift of Phra Pin Klao, 1856
Harris Treaty Gifts
USNM # 94 (3992)
51 cm diameter × 7.6 cm depth

FIG 144

FIG 145

FIG 146

"1 BRASS DRUM" KAREN DRUM AND MALLETS
"กลองมโหรึกะเหรี่ยง"
Gift of Phra Pin Klao, 1856
Harris Treaty Gifts
USNM # 70 (3991)

DETAIL, TYMPANUM
"1 Brass Drum" Karen drum and sticks
Gift of Phra Pin Klao, 1856
Harris Treaty Gifts
USNM # 70 (3991)

The Karen are a hill-tribe people who live to-day on the border between Thailand and Bur-ma, in the past in an outlying area between the Thai and the Burmese courts. The Karen were in a tributary relationship with the Thais, and were obligated to supply the court with brass drums and certain forest products. Karen drums are similar to the ancient Dongson Drums made in the Red River Valley region of Vietnam and traded to many areas of Asia, and perhaps represent an unbroken tradition of lost-wax casting of large ceremonial drums. In a thorough examination of nearly two hundred Karen drums and the history of such drums, Richard Cooler cites much evidence that these drums were in fact actually made by Shan craftsmen living in Karen areas. This drum is a "one-frog" drum, meaning that the four frogs on the tympanum are single, not stacks of two, three, or four frogs. The tympanum contains a 12-pointed central star and concentric bands of designs. This drum is rather plain; it does not include the rice-sheaf "tree-of-life" motif or marching elephants on the sides common to Karen drums. Karen drums were highly valued by the Thai court, and were used to announce the presence of the King.[100]

---

[100] Cooler 1986, Fraser-Lu, 1983.

THE THAI ORCHESTRA

King Mongkut gave Franklin Pierce a Javanese-style oboe (*pi chawa*), an important orchestral instrument, and King Chulalongkorn presented sets of orchestral instruments for the Siam Exhibit at the 1876 Centennial Exposition. These orchestras were an important feature of daily court life. Not only did the orchestras play for concerts and theatrical presentations, they often provided a musical background for court activities.

Thai classical musical system is thought to derive from Javanese court music. Certainly some of the instruments are also found in Javanese orchestras, particularly the *gong wong yai*, very close in form to Javanese gamelan gongs, and the reed instrument *pi*. However, the Javanese system is pentatonic, having five notes to the scale, while the Thai system has seven, with a true diatonic scale. Until recently, there was no written system of notation for Thai music. Students learned pieces by listening and imitating their teachers, and the entire musical tradition was passed on orally by teachers and through actual performance of pieces from memory.

SIAMESE VIOLIN AND BOW
"สีซอ"
Si So
Gift of King Chulalongkorn, 1876
Siam Exhibit, Centennial Exposition
USNM # 27311 (54066)
18.5 cm width × 47 cm length

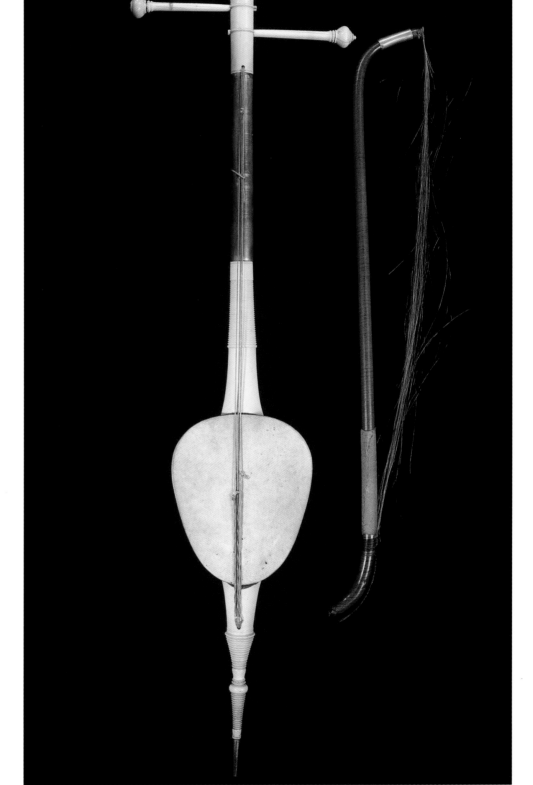

FIG 147

FIG 149

PAIR OF MALAY DRUMS
"กลอง"
Klong Malayu
Gift of King Chulalongkorn, 1876
Siam Exhibit, Centennial Exposition
USNM # 27315
53 cm height × 18.5 cm diameter

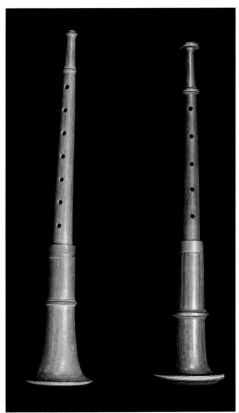

FIG 148

▲ JAVANESE FLUTE
"ปี่ฉวา"(ปี่ชวา)
Pi chawa
Gift of King Chulalongkorn, 1876
Siam Exhibit, Centennial Exposition
USNM # 27313 (54067)
37 cm length × 6 cm diameter of bell

JAVANESE-STYLE OBOE ▲
"ปี่ฉวา"(ปี่ชวา)
Pi chawa
Gift of King Mongkut, 1856
Harris Treaty Gifts
USNM # 77 (4001)
37 cm length × 6 cm diameter of bell

DRUM HELD BETWEEN THE KNEES
"โทน"
Gift of King Chulalongkorn, 1876
Siam Exhibit, Centennial Exposition
USNM # 27307

FIG 151

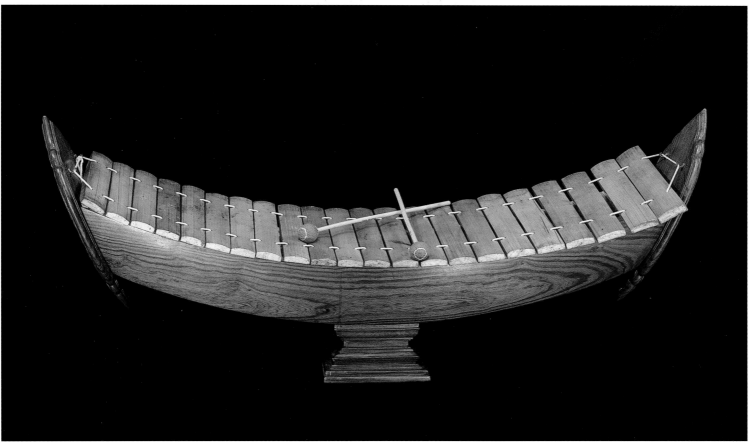

FIG 152

SIAMESE XYLOPHONE
"ระนาดทุ้ม"
Ranad thum
Gift of King Chulalongkorn, 1876
Siam Exhibit, Centennial Exposition
USNM # 27320 (54077)
117 cm length × 47 cm height × 37 cm depth

HAND DRUM
"รำมนา"
Ram mana
Gift of King Chulalongkorn, 1876
Siam Exhibit, Centennial Exposition
USNM # 27308 (54078)
28 cm diameter × 7 cm depth

FIG 150

FIG 153

130

8. THEATRICAL ARTS

The *khon* masked dance-dramas and *nang yai* and *nang talung* shadow puppet plays were very popular in Thailand in the nineteenth century and the *Ramakien* epic often provided the theatrical subject. The *Ramakien* epic represents a great battle for control of the world between the forces of good and evil. The cast of characters include humans, gods, monkeys, and demons. Humans, led by the heroic King Rama, are aided in the battle by their allies the monkeys and by certain gods against the forces of evil, the demons, led by the great ten-headed demon *Thotsakan.*

Khon dramas are often likened to the Western ballet, but in fact since the *khon* dances are choreographed with hundreds of set poses, each of which communicates a separate meaning, it is quite a bit more complex than the plot-based Western ballet.[101] Characters are divided into many groups, depending on the faction they represent, and whether they are human, simian, divine, or demon, and the color and shape of their masks and crowns represent these characteristics.

Khon masks are made of light paper-mâché and leather, with painted features and inlaid glass and mirrors. These masks are made only to last a few seasons, and are constantly repaired. The Smithsonian's collection of these masks is, however, remarkably well-preserved. New masks are made by faithfully following every detail of the old masks. The masks made by today's *khon* master mask makers look identical to these one hundred twenty-year-old masks.

◄ MASK OF *SUKHRIP* THE RED MONKEY KING OF KHITKHIN, ALLY OF RAMA,
"หน้าสุครีบ"(สุครีพ)
Na Sukhrip
Pavilion Army
Paper-mâché, paint, mirrors, and glass
Gift of King Chulalongkorn, 1876
Centennial Exposition, Siam Exhibit
USNM # 27377 (54233)
58 cm height × 26 cm width × 24 cm depth

---

[101] Yupho 1992.

131

**MASK OF WHITE MONKEY KING
HANUMAN**
"หน้าหนุมาณ"(หนุมาน)
Na Hanuman.
Pavilion Army
Paper-mâché, paint, mirrors, and glass
Gift of King Chulalongkorn, 1876
Centennial Exposition, Siam Exhibit
USNM # 27378
22 cm height × 24 cm width × 25 cm depth

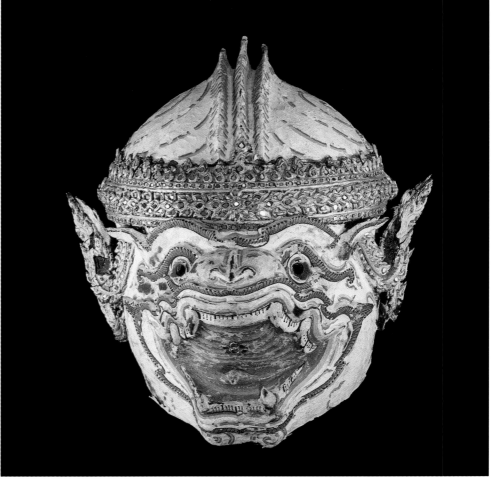

FIG 154

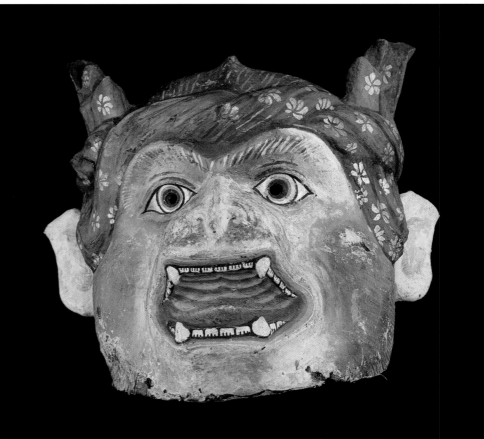

MASK OF MONKEY
"หน้าลิง"
Na Ling
Pavilion Army
Paper-mâché, paint, mirrors, and glass
Gift of King Chulalongkorn, 1876
Centennial Exposition, Siam Exhibit
USNM # 27381
21.5 cm height × 27 cm width × 26 cm depth

FIG 155

FIG 156

FIG 157

MASK OF GREEN 10-HEADED DEMON,
THOTSAKAN
"หน้าทศกรรฐ"
Na Thotsakan
Longka Army
Paper-mâché, paint, mirrors, and glass
Gift of King Chulalongkorn, 1876
Centennial Exposition, Siam Exhibit
USNM # 27382 (54232)
57 cm height × 28 cm width × 23 cm depth

MASK OF GREEN 10-HEADED DEMON,
THOTSAKAN
"หน้าทศกรรฐ"
Na Thotsakan
Detail of topmost head
Longka Army
Paper-mâché, paint, mirrors, and glass
Gift of King Chulalongkorn, 1876
Centennial Exposition, Siam Exhibit
USNM # 27382 (54232)

133

FIG 159

MASK OF GREEN DEMON
"หน้าอินทรชิต"
Na Inthrachit
Paper-mâché, paint, mirrors, and glass
Gift of King Chulalongkorn, 1876
Centennial Exposition, Siam Exhibit
USNM # 27384 (54240)
62 cm height × 23 cm width × 23 cm depth

FIG 158

MASK OF THE GREEN DEMON PHIPHEK
"หน้าพิเภก"
Na Phiphek
Longka Army
Paper-mâché, paint, mirrors, and glass
Gift of King Chulalongkorn, 1876
Centennial Exposition, Siam Exhibit
USNM # 27383 (54239)
55 cm height × 29 cm width × 24 cm depth

FIG 160

FIG 161

FIG 162

MASK OF *ONGKOT* ▲
"หน้าองคต"
Na Ongkhot
Longka Army
Paper-mâché, paint, mirrors, and glass
Gift of King Chulalongkorn, 1876
Centennial Exposition, Siam Exhibit
USNM # 27379 (54238)
44 cm height × 27 cm width × 26 cm depth

MASK OF VERMILLION DEMON *SATASUN*
Lord of Atsadong, friend of *Thotsakan*
"หน้าสะตสูร"
Na Satasun
Longka Army
Paper-mâché, paint, mirrors, and glass
Gift of King Chulalongkorn, 1876
Centennial Exposition, Siam Exhibit
USNM # 27385 (54235)
43 cm height × 26 cm width × 28 cm depth

MASK OF BROWN DEMON NEPHEW OF THOTSAKAN
"หน้าวิรุญจำบัง'
Na Wirun cham bang
Longka Army
Paper-mâché, paint, mirrors, and glass
Gift of King Chulalongkorn, 1876
Centennial Exposition, Siam Exhibit
USNM # 27386
25 cm height × 30 cm width × 25 cm depth

135

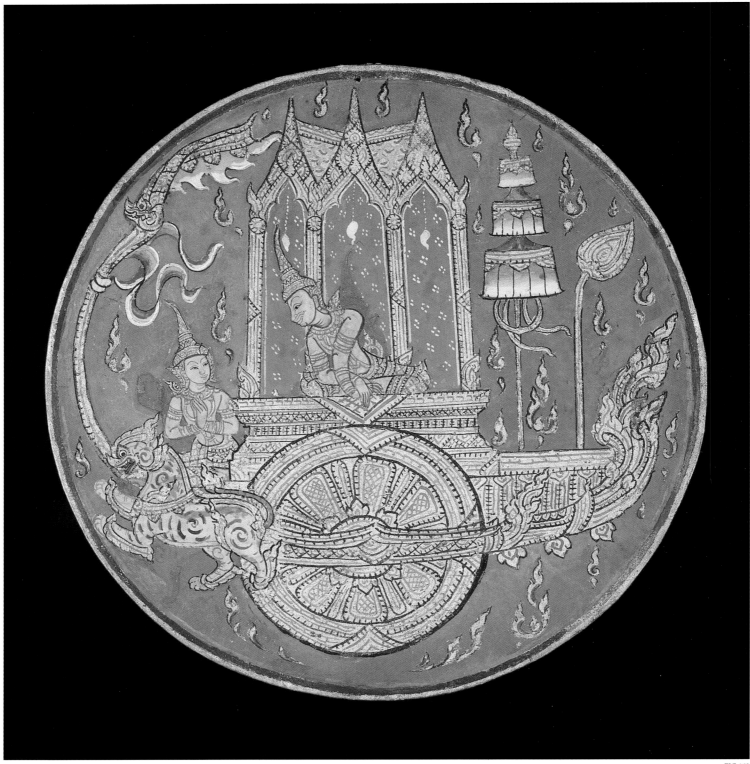

FIG 163

THE NANG YAI SHADOW PUPPET PLAYS

There are two forms of shadow puppetry in Thailand. The *Nang Yai* and the *Nang Ta-Lung*. *Nang Ta-Lung* are movable figures and resemble the *Wayang Kulit* puppets of Indonesian Courts. These Siamese shadow puppet plays were heavily influenced by shadow puppetry on the Malay Peninsula. The more common *Nang Yai* are larger figures, sometimes up to six feet tall. The figures are cut from buffalo hide, except for the *rusi*, the yogi figure which is cut from tiger hide to impart it with magical powers. Thai shadow puppets are not as highly decorated as their Indonesian counterparts, but these were probably used for the performances held during the late afternoon and into dusk as well, since they are painted.[102] Shadow puppet performances began in the late afternoon and often lasted often until dawn of the next day.

Shadow puppetry was originally a southern Thai tradition, and performances were often presented in largely Southern dialect, while royal characters spoke in central Thai dialect and in royal language. The puppet plays often went on through the night, and the main plot was at times punctuated by political and risqué humor. The leather is thick and painted with colorful accents that can only be seen in daylight. Shadow puppets for evening performances were thinner and more transparent.[103] There were often hundreds of puppets in a puppet show master's collection, and many stories were performed, including many derived from the *Ramakien.*

Pre-Performance Invocations and skits

The shadow puppet figure of a buffoon, *Nang Talok,* was used in a comical pre-performance curtain-raiser, where he intervenes in a battle between a white monkey and a black monkey. In the late afternoon before any theatrical presentation, ritual offerings are given to the theater teachers and to deities of the Hindu cosmology. Sometimes, aside from the comical skit with monkeys and the buffoon, other short skits such as a dance of the seasons were performed, as represented by the small model figures of larger shadow puppets, *Ramasoon* and *Nang Mekhala,* which were used to act out the violent fighting which produces thunder and lighting, the thunder by the action of *Ramasoon's* battle axe, and the lighting by the action of the flashing of *Nang Mekhala's* magical crystal sphere as they chase one another through the heavens.[104] *Phra Chant*, the moon god, and *Phra Ahtit* , the sun god also played a part in these dances of the seasons, and the Smithsonian's set of round paintings of these nature gods came with instructions for mounting them on the stage.

The style of painting here is very much like Thai mural painting. The figures are seen in traditional poses, and were probably made from standard stencils, which the artist would have used to chalk an outline of each figure. The artist would then have filled in the colored details, again following the strict stylistic guidelines of Thai classical painting.

◄ **PAINTING OF THE SUN GOD**
"ดวงพระอาทิตย์"
Dwang Phra Ahtit
Paint on canvas, mounted on tin
Gift of King Chulalongkorn, 1876
Centennial Exposition, Siam Exhibit
USNM # 27208 (T-1978A)
(1 of 2)
24 cm diameter

---

[102] Smithies and Kerdchouay 1972.
[103] Smithies and Kerdchouay, 1972, pp. 129-134.
[104] Wray et al 1979

137

PAIR OF PAINTINGS OF THE MOON GOD
"ดวงพระจันทร์"
Dwang Phra chan
Paint on canvas, mounted on tin
Gift of King Chulalongkorn, 1876
Siam exhibit, Centennial Exposition
USNM # 27209 (T-1378C)
24 cm diameter

FIG 164

FIG 165

138

**PAINTED SHADOW PUPPET OF
THUNDER GOD**
"รามสูร"
Ramasoon
Painted leather
Gift of King Chulalongkorn, 1876
Centennial Exposition, Siam Exhibit
USNM # 27211 (T1377C)
28 cm height × 21 cm width

FIG 167

**PAINTED SHADOW PUPPET OF
LIGHTNING GODDESS**
"นางเมฆขลา"
Nang Mekh Khla
Painted leather
Gift of King Chulalongkorn, 1876
Centennial Exposition, Siam Exhibit
USNM # 27210 (T1377A)
30 cm height × 21 cm width

FIG 166

139

FIG 168

SHADOW PUPPET OF A BUFFOON
"หนังตะหลก"(ตลก)
Nang Talok
Painted leather
Gift of King Chulalongkorn, 1876
Centennial Exposition, Siam Exhibit
USNM # 27220 T8888 # 1
78 cm height × 25 cm width

FIG 169

NANG YAI SHADOW PUPPETS

2 DEMONS IN A CHARIOT.
Thotsakan and another *Yak*
"หนังยักมี"(หนังยักษ์)
Nang Yak
Painted leather
Gift of King Chulalongkorn, 1876
Centennial Exposition, Siam Exhibit
USNM # 27216 (T8888 # 2)
68 cm height × 51 cm width

RAMA AND LAKSMA ▶
"หนังพระราม"
Nang Phra Ram
Painted leather
Gift of King Chulalongkorn, 1876
Centennial Exposition, Siam Exhibit
USNM # 27217 (T8887 # 8)
90 cm height × 63 cm width

140

FIG 170

FIG 172

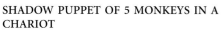

FIG 171

FIG 173

SHADOW PUPPET OF 5 MONKEYS IN A CHARIOT
"หนังเขนลิง"
Nang khan ling
Gift of King Chulalongkorn, 1876
Centennial Exposition, Siam Exhibit
USNM # 27218 (T8888 # 11)
68 cm height × 51 cm width

HANUMAN, **THE WHITE MONKEY KING ATOP ENEMY**
หนุมาน
Hanuman
Painted leather
Gift of King Chulalongkorn, 1876
Centennial Exposition, Siam Exhibit
USNM # 27218 (T8888 # 4)
66 cm height × 27 cm width

HEROINE OF THE RAMAKIEN (*SIDA*)
"หนังนาง"
Nang nang
Gift of King Chulalongkorn, 1876
Centennial Exposition, Siam Exhibit
USNM # 27219 (T8888 # 21)
78 cm height × 25 cm width

143

FIG 174

144

9. EVERYDAY LIFE

King Chulalongkorn sent a carefully composed exhibit to represent his nation in the 1876 Centennial Exposition held in Philadelphia to celebrate the Centennial of American independence. The "Siam Exhibit" was quite large: it consisted of over 900 items representing a wide variety of aspects of nineteenth-century Thai life. A truly comprehensive exhibit, it contained everything from elegant mother-of-pearl-inlaid masterpieces and *Khon* masks to fishing boat models and woodworking tools. The exhibit was shown in the Navy Department section of the U.S. Government Building. The entire exhibit was a gift to President Ulysses S. Grant and the people of the United States from King Chulalongkorn and was turned over to the Smithsonian Institution.[105]

Some years later King Chulalongkorn learned of the Smithsonian's efforts to study basketry of the world, and he sent some additional baskets and fish traps in 1881, at the time of the ratification of revisions to the Harris Treaty.

The "Siam Exhibit" at the Louisiana Purchase Exposition of 1904 was even more elaborate than the earlier Centennial Exposition. The Thais built their own pavilion, a beautiful building modeled after the striking Wat Benjamabobit, the "Marble Temple" completed in Bangkok in 1899. The pavilion housed mostly objects related to Buddhism, music, literary life, and theater. Other Thai objects were housed in general exhibition buildings at the exposition; over six hundred pieces were exhibited in the Fish and Game, Manufactures and Mines, and Agriculture sections.[106]

In these more general halls, the Thais chose to exhibit many items and processes from daily economic pursuits of its population. Expositions were trade shows as well as cultural exhibits and the Thai commissioners hoped to promote their fishing, textile, lumber, mining, and basketry industries.[107] These items were presented to the President of the United States as gifts from the King Chulalongkorn, and are now in the Smithsonian's ethnology collections. These include baskets, fish traps, models of agricultural machines, fishing boat models, and agricultural tools.

◄ NORTHEAST THAI (LAO) STICKY RICE CONTAINER.
"กระติบข้าวเหนียว"
Kratip Khaoniaw
Bamboo, wood, and paint
Gift of King Chulalongkorn, 1904
Siam Exhibit, Louisiana Purchase Exposition
USNM # 234035
47 cm height × 14 cm diameter

This Lao sticky-rice container from Udon, in northeast Thailand, is footed in almost the same manner as the traditional Thai ceramic raised dish. Its red-painted wooden elements are reminiscent of architectural wood carvings of the northeast. The split-bamboo basketry portion of the piece is double layered to provide insulation for hot rice. The outer layer is plaited in a diagonal herringbone pattern, while the inner layer is plaited on the bottom and twined at the top. The lid is plaited in a single layer and edged with red cotton cloth. The pinnacle of carved flowers rises to a central spire. Baskets such as this are used for serving the glutinous rice used in northeastern Thai cuisine. Main dishes are usually served in ceramic or enameled metal bowls while the sticky rice is served in a communal container such as this one. The meal is served in the center of a floor mat, and diners seat themselves in the form of a circle on the mat. Diners reach into the container for a small portion of rice, form it into a concave scoop in their fingers and then use this rice "spoon" to scoop up a bite of the main dish.

[105] U.S. Navy 1876.
[106] Carter 1904.
[107] Gerini 1912.

FIG 175

BASKETRY-TRAY WITH SPOTTED BAMBOO TRIM AND *DOK PIKUN* FLOWER DESIGN.
"ตะแกรงดอกพิกุน"
Ta kræng dok pikun
Bamboo
Gift of King Chulalongkorn, 1876
Siam Exhibit, Centennial Exposition
USNM # 27176 (T-1550)
41 cm width × 10 cm height

FIG 176

Thai Basketry

Basketry was an integral part of life in nineteenth century Siam, and still has a place of importance in rural Thailand. Locally available weaving supplies were a convenient source for woven containers of a myriad of styles, shapes, and functions. Some of the basket styles represented in the Smithsonian's Thai collections are styles that are common to many parts of Asia, but the majority of them are uniquely Southeast Asian, and uniquely Thai.

FLOWER BASKET WITH HANDLE AND SPOTTED BAMBOO TRIM.
"กเช้าดอกไม้"(กระเช้าดอกไม้)
Ka chao dok mai
(more commonly *Kra chao dok mai*)[108]
Bamboo
Gift of King Chulalongkorn, 1876
Siam Exhibit, Centennial Exposition
USNM # 27177
15 cm height (height of handle 32 cm) × 26 cm width × 35 cm length

This elegant hexagonal basket has a coiled and stitched handle and a latticework body in the *dok pikun* flower (*Mimusops elengi*) motif. The trim is of a highly prized mottled bamboo.

MARKET BASKET WITH SPOTTED BAMBOO TRIM
"กระบุง"
Kra bung
Bamboo
Gift of King Chulalongkorn, 1904
Siam Exhibit, Louisiana Purchase Exposition
USNM # 235913
42 cm diameter at rim × 32 cm height

[108] McFarland 1944, pp. 25

FIG 177

BASKET FOR TRANSPORTING VEGETABLES AND OTHER GOODS TO MARKET
"กจาด"(กระจาด)
Kra jat.[109]
Bamboo, rattan
Gift of King Chulalongkorn, 1876
Siam Exhibit, Centennial Exposition
USNM # 27180
37 cm diameter × 32 cm height

FIG 178

OPENWORK BASKET FOR WASHING ARTICLES
"ตะกร้าชำระ"
Ta kra cham ra[110]
Gift of King Chulalongkorn, 1876
Siam Exhibit, Centennial Exposition
USNM # 27195
32 cm diameter × 14 cm height

FIG 179

COILED *YAEN LIPHAO* FERN-VINE BETEL BOX[111]
"กล่องสำหรับใส่หมาก"
Klong samrap sai mak
Gift of King Chulalongkorn, 1876
Siam Exhibit, Centennial Exposition
USNM # 27197
20 cm diameter × 15 cm height

This light-colored betel box is delicately patterned, yet sturdy. It is meant to sit on a base decorated with a broad band of the darker fern-vine and an elegantly executed set of woven split bamboo pillars woven into the split bamboo base.

[109] McFarland 1944, p. 20.
[110] *Ta Kra*; McFarland 1944, p. 349. *Cham ra* McFarland 1944, p. 295.
[111] Annez 1994, pp. 142-151.

FIG 180

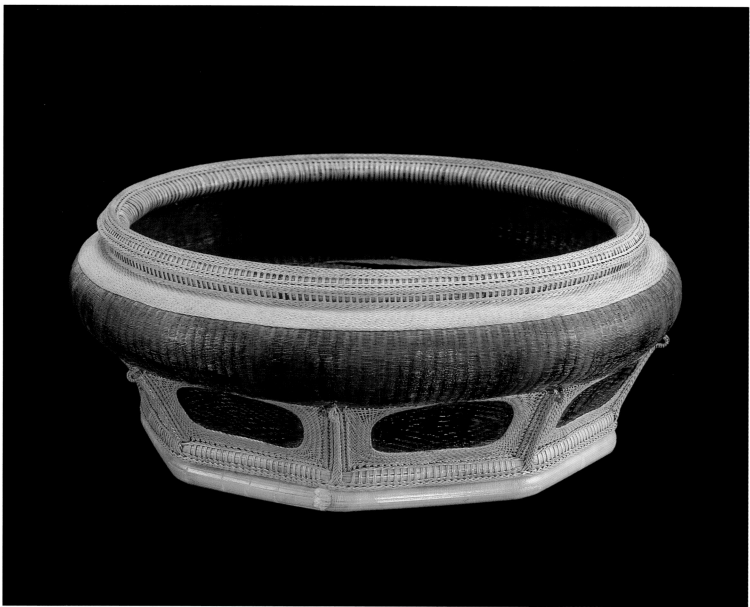

FIG 181

BETEL BOX STAND
"รองกล่องสำหรับใส่หมาก"
Rong klong samrap sai mak
Gift of King Chulalongkorn, 1876
Siam Exhibit, Centennial Exposition
USNM # 27179
20 cm diameter × 17 cm height

FIG 182

The *Yæn Liphao Yai* fern vine (*Schizaeceae*) is used to create some of the most intricate and elegant basketry in Southeast Asia. In Thailand, both the tan and nearly black varieties are used to great effect. The vines are split into three strands, dried, and then sewn around a coiled rattan base. This unique type of basketry has been revived and promoted by Her Majesty, Queen Sirikit through a training and marketing program known as the SUPPORT Foundation.[112]

▲BETEL BASKETS
"กล่องสำหรับใส่หมาก"
Klong samrap sai mak
Gift of King Chulalongkorn, 1876
Siam Exhibit, Centennial Exposition
Gift of King Chulalongkorn, 1904
Siam Exhibit, Louisiana Purchase Exposition
USNM #s 227197, 34036, 234037

[112] Annez 1994, pp. 142-151.

FIG 183

150

FIG 184

◄ *YÆN LIPHAO YAI* FERN-VINE BETEL
BOX
"กล่องสำหรับใส่หมาก"
Klong samrap sai mak
Gift of King Chulalongkorn, 1904
Siam Exhibit, Louisiana Purchase Exposition
USNM # 234037
21 cm diameter × 11.5 cm height

This betel box uses all of the classic methods and designs of traditional *Yæn Liphao Yai* fern vine basketry. The extreme regularity of the stitches is achieved by first splitting and then pulling the strands of vine through a metal die, giving each strand used the identical diameter. The structure of the box is formed by use of a single stitch carried over two rattan coils at a time. The subtle color gradients are achieved by using different varieties of the vine, and both the dark and light elements are carried vertically row by row. Stitches are eliminated and added as called for by the pattern. The pattern used here is a mixture of delicate diamonds and bold triangles. The main element in the central band of the body is the "rice ball pattern."

▲*YÆN LIPHAO YAI* FERN VINE BETEL
BOX.
Inner basket with diamond and horse motifs
Gift of King Chulalongkorn, 1904
Siam Exhibit, Louisiana Purchase Exposition
USNM # 234036
9 cm length × 6.5 cm width × 2.5 cm
thickness

FIG 186

▲ PAIR OF MINIATURE MARKET BASKETS
Gift of Queen Sirikit to the Smithsonian
Institution, 1982
USNM # 421962,
10.5 cm height × 13 cm diameter
USNM # 421963
10.3 cm height × 12 cm diameter

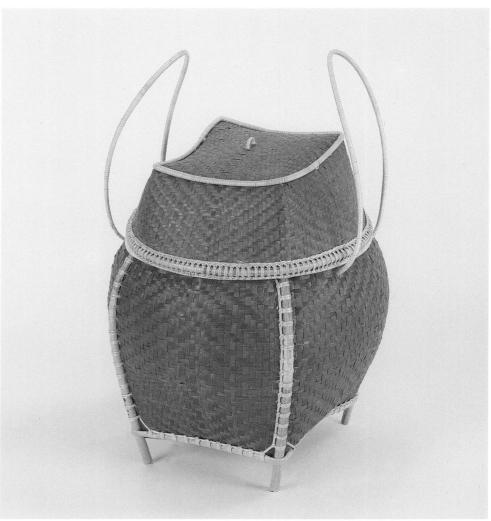

COVERED STICKY RICE BASKET
Gift of Queen Sirikit to the Smithsonian
Institution, 1982
USNM # 421964
19 cm height × 14.5 cm diameter

FIG 187

FIG 185

SHALLOW BASKET
Gift of Queen Sirikit to the Smithsonian
Institution, 1982
USNM # 421961
10.5 cm height × 27.5 cm diameter

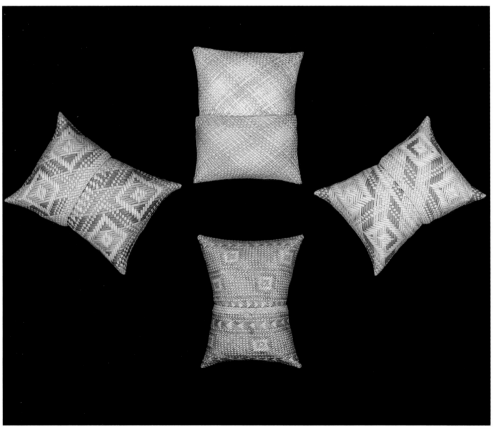

FIG 188

TOBACCO OR BETEL CONTAINERS
"ตลับยาสูบ"
Talap ya sup
Gift of King Chulalongkorn, 1904
Louisiana Purchase Exposition
USNM # 234039
Ranging from 8.5 cm to 9.5 cm length × 5.5
to 7.5 cm width × 2.5 cm to 3.5 cm thick

These small basketry containers are mini-
samplers of Thai mat-making technology and
motifs.

153

MAT WITH BOLD BOX PATTERNS IN EGGPLANT PURPLE
"เสื่อหวาย"
Su'a wai
Rattan
Gift of King Chulalongkorn, 1904
Louisiana Purchase Exposition
USNM # 235016
66 cm width × 155 cm length

FIG 190

FIG 191

MATS

Thai people use mats for many purposes. Today even remote village houses have highly polished teak floors, some dating back to the nineteenth century–and these floors are hand-polished and treated as family heirlooms. Mats protect fine teak floors when the house is used for a work area, such as for preparing food, or when meals are served. The traditional Thai house has little furniture, and the mats serve for both seating and tables. Bedding is also placed atop mats, and the whole of the bedding is folded or rolled and set aside during the day. Perhaps because of its role in sleeping, since prehistoric times mats have been used to wrap the corpse, either for burial in earlier times or cremation in the Buddhist era.

This selection of mats from the dozens sent to the Louisiana Purchase Exposition is meant to convey the broad range of mat styles available in Thailand in the nineteenth century. These mats are made of a variety of materials; bamboo from the central region, using both natural and chemical dyes and sometimes with cloth strips woven in, and pandanus leaf from the south. Designs range from simple undyed weaves, undyed but complexly patterned weaves, to dyed stripes and jaunty dyed animals from the Asian horoscope.[113]

Today most Thai mats are made of plastic by machine. Though many of the traditional patterns are still used, the pleasing natural dyes found in these nineteenth-century mats are a thing of the past.

MAT WITH NATURAL AND PURPLE DESIGN
"เสื่อเตย"
Su'a Toei
Pandanus leaf
Gift of King Chulalongkorn, 1904
Louisiana Purchase Exposition
USNM # 236046
66 cm width × 134 cm width

MAT WITH BLACK AND WHITE CHECK PATTERN
"เสื่อเตย"
Su'a Toei
Pandanus Leaf
Gift of King Chulalongkorn, 1904
Louisiana Purchase Exposition
USNM # 235980
61 cm width × 178 cm length

FIG 189

[113] Robyn Maxwell and others look to mat designs as a holdover from early primitive beaten felted bark cloth. Indeed, many of the bold designs found on these pandanas mats are reminiscent of outer island Indonesian painted designs found on bark cloths (Maxwell 1992, pp. 26-29).

FIG 192

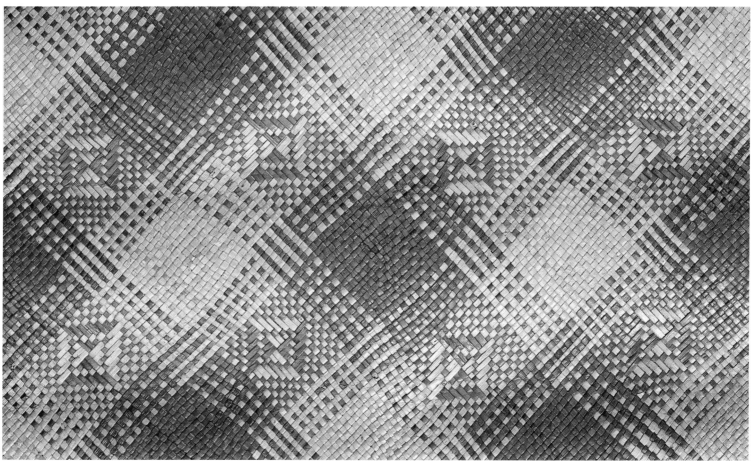

FIG 193

◄ MAT WITH PLAID PATTERN IN FADED
RED AND OLIVE
"เสื่อเตย"
Su'a Toei
Pandanus leaf
Gift of King Chulalongkorn, 1904
Louisiana Purchase Exposition
USNM # 235984
51 cm width × 162 cm length

MAT WITH SUBTLE *MUD MEE* DESIGN
IN GREEN AND YELLOW, WITH PURPLE
BORDER
"เสื่อหวาย"
Su'a wai
Rattan
Gift of King Chulalongkorn, 1904
Louisiana Purchase Exposition
USNM # 235979
51 cm width × 81 cm length

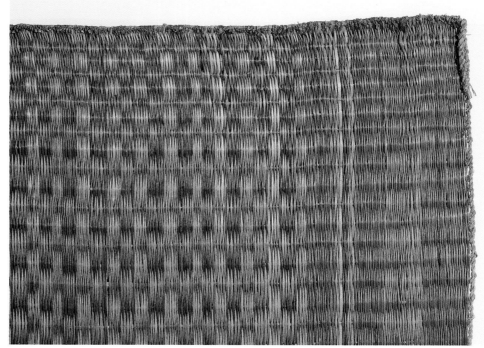

FIG 194

◄ MAT WITH YELLOW AND BURGUNDY
PLAID PATTERN
"เสื่อเตย"
Su'a Toei
Pandanus leaf
Gift of King Chulalongkorn, 1904
Louisiana Purchase Exposition
USNM # 235991
56 cm width × 160 cm length

MAT WITH SUPPLEMENTARY COTTON
THREADS INTERWOVEN
"เสื่อหวาย"
Su'a wai
Rattan and cotton threads
Gift of King Chulalongkorn, 1904
Louisiana Purchase Exposition
USNM # 236049
102 cm length × 180 cm length

FIG 195

157

FIG 196

FIG 197

FIG 198

◄ MAT WITH GEOMETRIC PATTERN AND
RED CLOTH BACKING
"เสื่อเตย"
Su'a Toei
Pandanus leaf
Gift of King Chulalongkorn, 1904
Louisiana Purchase Exposition
USNM # 236047
61 cm width × 170 cm length

◄ MAT WITH GEOMETRIC PATTERN AND
RED CLOTH BORDER
"เสื่อเตย"
Su'a Toei
Pandanus leaf and cotton cloth
Gift of King Chulalongkorn, 1904
Louisiana Purchase Exposition
USNM # 235042

◄ DETAIL–PANDANUS LEAF MAT WITH
GEOMETRIC PATTERN AND RED CLOTH
BORDER
Gift of King Chulalongkorn, 1904
Louisiana Purchase Exposition
USNM # 235042

MAT WITH ASTROLOGICAL SIGN: RATS
"เสื่อหวาย"
Su'a wai
Rattan
Gift of King Chulalongkorn, 1904
Louisiana Purchase Exposition
USNM # 235966
61 cm width × 188 cm length

FIG 199

159

MAT WITH ASTROLOGICAL SIGN: ROOSTER
"เสื่อหวาย"
Su'a wai
Rattan
Gift of King Chulalongkorn, 1904
Louisiana Purchase Exposition
USNM # 235967
86 cm width × 188 cm length

FIG 200

FIG 201

COTTON TEXTILES AND
COTTON GIN

COTTON GIN
"หีบปั่นฝ้าย"
Hip pan fai
Wood and steel
Gift of King Chulalongkorn, 1904
Louisiana Purchase Exposition
USNM # 235418
42 cm width × 61 cm height

161

SQUIRREL-TAIL (MULTI-HUED TWISTED WARP) WEAVE COTTON
"ผ้าหางกระรอก"
Pha Hang Krarok
Cotton
Gift of King Chulalongkorn, 1876
Centennial Exposition
USNM # 27132
85 cm width × 155 cm width

FIG 202

SQUIRREL-TAIL (MULTI-HUED TWISTED WARP) WEAVE COTTON
"ผ้าหางกระรอก"
Pha Hang Krarok
Cotton
Gift of King Chulalongkorn, 1876
Centennial Exposition
USNM # 27388
109 cm length × 89 cm width

FIG 203

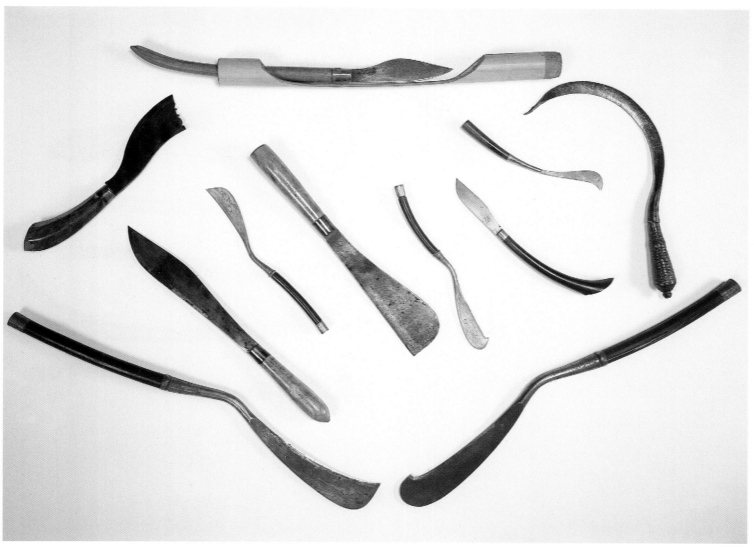

FIG 204

AGRICULTURAL TOOLS

**VARIETY OF KNIVES, MACHETES,
AND SICKLES**
Steel and wood
Gifts of King Chulalongkorn, 1904
Siam Exhibit, Louisiana Purchase Exposition
USNM #s 236089, 236093 (2 items), 236107,
236121 (2 items), 236124

VARIETY OF KNIVES, MACHETES, AND SICKLES
Steel and wood
Gift of King Chulalongkorn, 1904
Siam Exhibit, Louisiana Purchase Exposition
USNM #s 236089, 236124
From 30 cm to 74 cm length

SET OF KNIVES
Steel and wood
Gift of King Chulalongkorn, 1904
Siam Exhibit, Louisiana Purchase Exposition
USNM # 236093
From 35.5 cm length to 53 cm length

These knives are all hand wrought and set into fine hardwood. Knives such as these are used in agricultural work, craftwork, and food preparation.

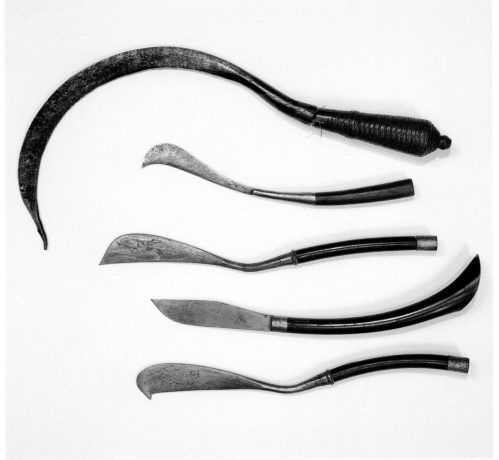

FIG 205

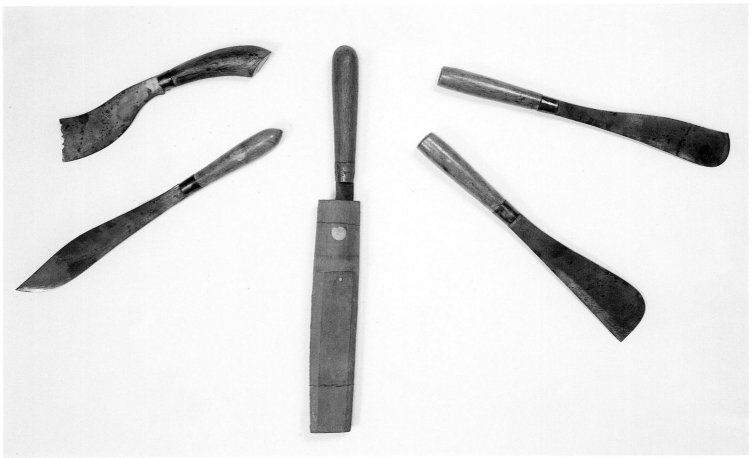

FIG 206

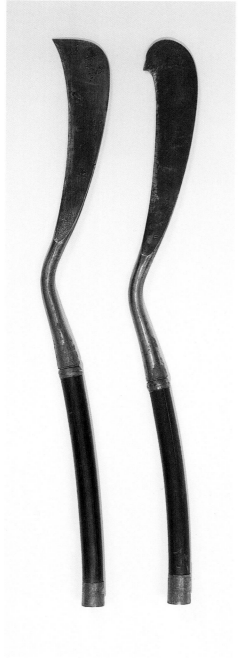

FIG 207

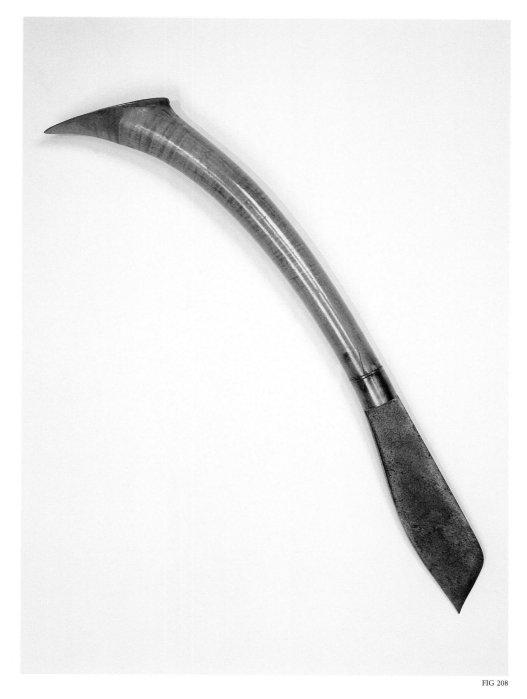

FIG 208

PAIR OF LONG KNIVES
"มีดขอ"
Mit kho'
Steel and wood
Gift of King Chulalongkorn, 1904
Louisiana Purchase Exposition
USNM # 236121

MACHETE
"มีดตอก"
Mit tok
Steel and wood
Gift of King Chulalongkorn, 1904
Louisiana Purchase Exposition
USNM # 236097
51 cm length

KNIFE
"มีดโต้"
Mit to
Steel and wood
Gift of King Chulalongkorn, 1904
Louisiana Purchase Exposition
USNM # 236095
33 cm length

FIG 209

KNIFE
Detail of blade
See: Fig. 209, above

FIG 210

FIG 211

MACHETE
"มีดตอก"
Mit tok
Steel and wood
Gift of King Chulalongkorn, 1904
Louisiana Purchase Exposition
USNM # 236107
53 cm length

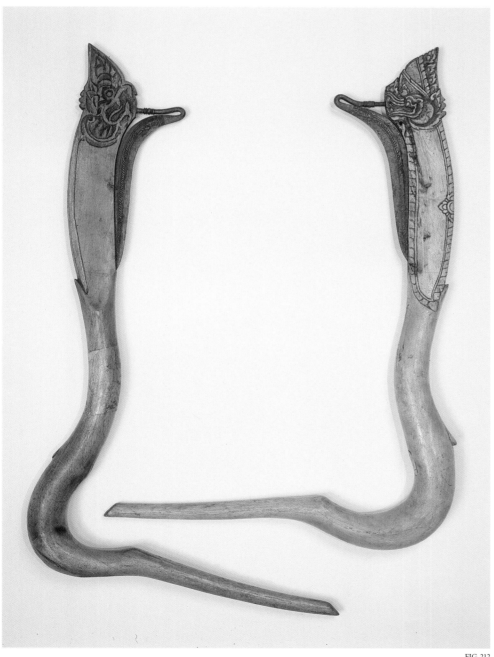

RICE SCYTHES
"มีดเคียว"
Mit Kiaw
Steel and wood
Gift of King Chulalongkorn, 1904
Siam Exhibit, Louisiana Purchase Exposition
USNM #s 236085, 236091
Each 45 cm length

FIG 212

167

DETAIL, RICE SCYTHE
"มีดเคียว"
Mit Kiaw
Gift of King Chulalongkorn, 1904
Siam Exhibit, Louisiana Purchase Exposition
USNM # 236085

DETAIL, RICE SCYTHE ▶
"มีดเคียว"
Mit Kiaw
Gift of King Chulalongkorn, 1904
Siam Exhibit, Louisiana Purchase Exposition
USNM # 236091

FIG 214

FIG 213

RICE MEASURE
"ถังตวงข้าว"
Tang tu'ang khao
Wood
Gift of King Chulalongkorn, 1904
Louisiana Purchase Exposition
USNM # 235910
20 cm diameter × 20 cm height

FIG 215

FIG 217

FIG 216

MODEL OF RICE WINNOWING MACHINE
"เครื่องสีข้าว"
Kru'ang si khao
Gift of King Chulalongkorn, 1904
Louisiana Purchase Exposition
USNM # 236058
26 cm length × 19 cm height
68 cm height × 51 cm width

BUCKET
"ถังน้ำ"
Tang nam
Wood, steel bands
Gift of King Chulalongkorn, 1904
Louisiana Purchase Exposition
USNM # 236053
23 cm diameter × 18 cm height

169

FIG 218

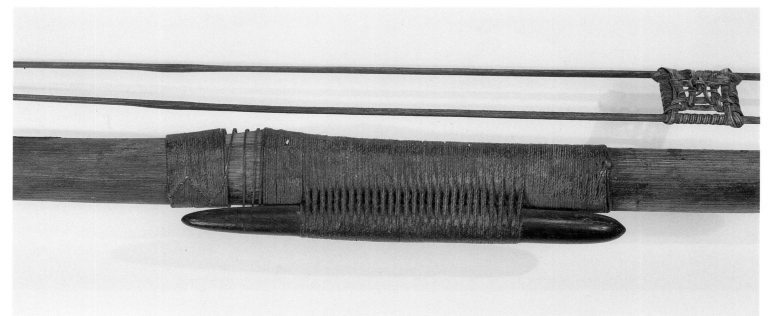

FIG 219

▲PELLET BOW
"ธนูยิงกระสุน"(หน้าไม้)
Tanu ying kra sun (Na mai)
Wood, fiber, horn
Gift of King Chulalongkorn, 1904
Louisiana Purchase Exposition
USNM # 235900
152 cm length

▲DETAIL OF LASHING ON GRIP OF
PELLET BOW
"ธนูยิงกระสุน"(หน้าไม้)
Tanu ying kra sun (Na mai)
Gift of King Chulalongkorn, 1904
Louisiana Purchase Exposition
USNM # 235900

PELLETS
"ลูกกระสุน"
Luk kra sun
Earthenware
USNM # 331950
1.8 cm diameter

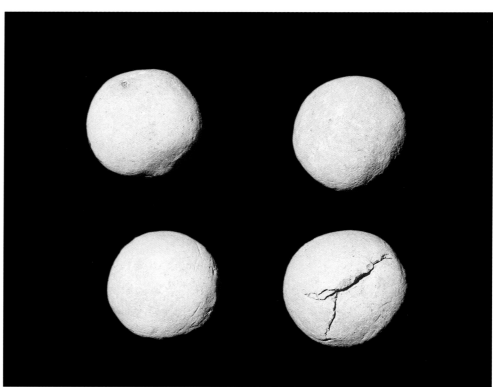

FIG 220

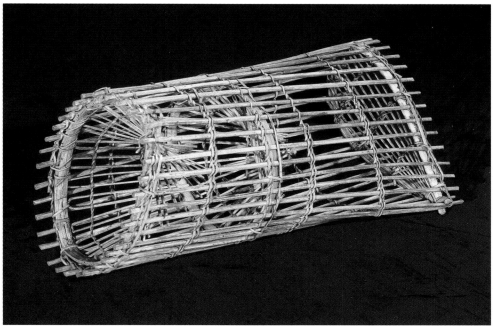

FIG 222

HUNTING AND FISHING

Siam had a booming fishing industry, and wished to promote the sale of salted and other preserved fish to the West. The Siam Exhibit at the Louisiana Purchase Exposition included dozens of fish traps, fishing nets, and fishing boat models which were arrayed in an impressive display. Hunting was represented by many animal pelts, mammal traps, bows and arrows, and pellet bows.

FISHING GEAR

FISH TRAP
"ลอบดักปลา"
Lop dak pla
Gift of King Chulalongkorn, 1904
Louisiana Purchase Exposition
USNM # 235794
13 cm width × 28 cm length

This type of trap is made to lay horizontally on the bottom. The fish swim in the side and cannot emerge.

FISH TRAP
"ตุ้ม"
Tum
Gift of King Chulalongkorn, 1904
Louisiana Purchase Exposition
USNM # 235787
122 cm length × 63.5 cm width

This kind of trap will stand upright in the water, resting on the bottom. Fish swim in the opening in the front, but sharp tines prevent their escape.

FIG 221

171

FIG 223

FISH TRAP
"สุ่ม"
Sum
Gift of King Chulalongkorn, 1904
Louisiana Purchase Exposition
USNM # 235765
25 cm diameter × 27.94 cm height

This type of trap is used by hand. As the trap is lowered by hand over the fish, the tines sink into the mud, trapping the fish.

FISH CREEL
"อีจู้"
Iju
Gift of King Chulalongkorn, 1904
Louisiana Purchase Exposition
USNM # 235753
13 cm diameter × 25.4 cm height

Creels are used for storing fish.

FISH TRAP
ไซ
Sai
Gift of King Chulalongkorn, 1904
Louisiana Purchase Exposition
USNM # 235651
12 cm diameter × 51 cm length.

FIG 224

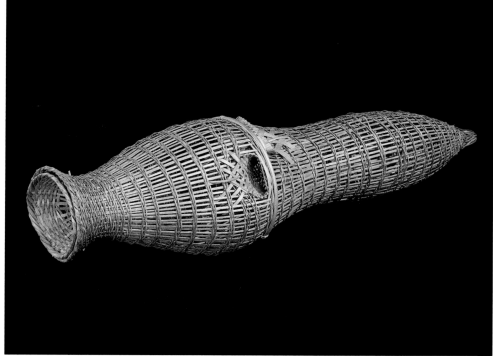

FIG 225

FIG 226

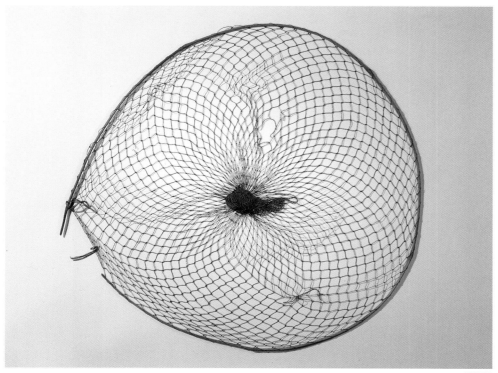

FIG 227

FISH CREEL
"อีเป็ด ข้องลอย"
I pet khong loy
Gift of King Chulalongkorn, 1904
Louisiana Purchase Exposition
USNM # 235674
30.5 cm length × 30.5 cm height

This creel can be floated alongside a person or a boat as fish are collected from the traps.

MODEL OF FISH NET
"สวิง"
Sa wing
Gift of King Chulalongkorn, 1904
Louisiana Purchase Exposition
USNM # 235825
51 cm diameter

173

**FISHING BOAT MODEL WITH
MINIATURE FISHING EQUIPMENT**
"เรือฉลอม"
Ru'a chalom
Gift of King Chulalongkorn, 1904
Louisiana Purchase Exposition
USNM # 235531
59.2 cm length 11 cm width

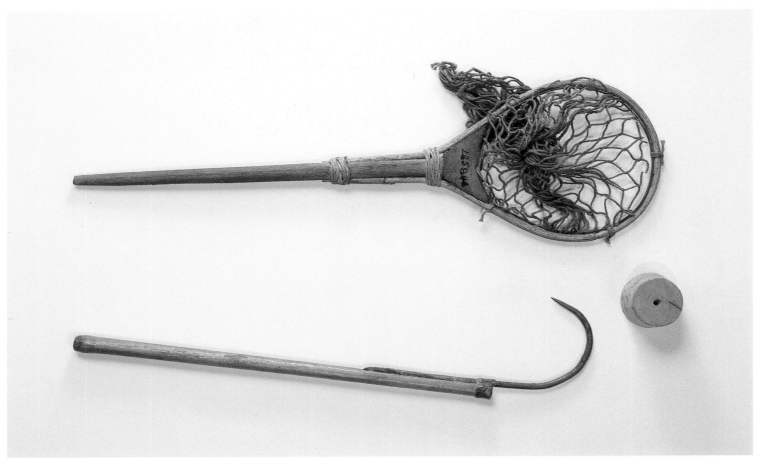

FIG 228

FIG 229

◄ MODEL OF FISH SCOOP AND
GRAPPLING HOOK
"ตาข่ายตักปลา"
Ta kai tak pla
Gift of King Chulalongkorn, 1904
Louisiana Purchase Exposition
USNM # 235896, 28 cm length
T 1409, 25 cm length

THAI HOUSE MODELS:
ON WATER AND LAND

HOUSE BOAT (*SAMPAN*) MODEL
"เรือสำปั้น"
Ru'a sampan
Gift of King Chulalongkorn, 1904
Louisiana Purchase Exposition
USNM # 160298
71.7 cm length × 15 cm width

176

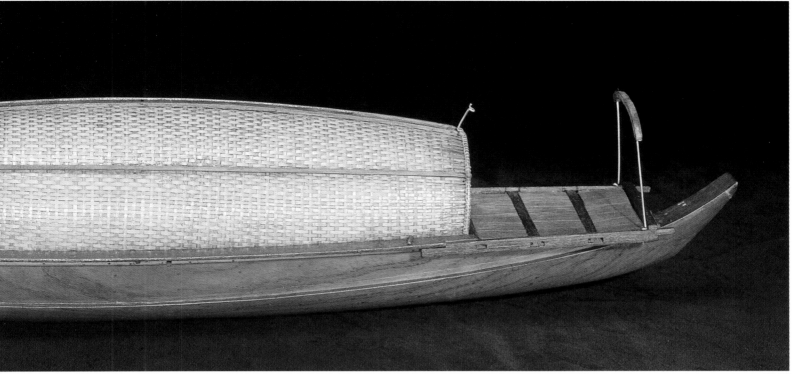

FIG 230

FIG 231

HOUSE BOAT (*SAMPAN*) MODEL
"เรือสำปั้น"
Ru'a sampan
Gift of King Chulalongkorn, 1904
Louisiana Purchase Exposition
USNM # 160314
56.3 cm length × 17.6 cm width

177

FIG 235

MODEL OF A NINETEENTH-CENTURY RURAL THAI HOUSE
"บ้านทรงไทย"
Ban song thai
Gift of King Chulalongkorn, 1876
Centennial Exposition, Siam Exhibit
USNM # 27372
35.5 cm height × 43 cm width

The basic model for the rural Thai house has changed little since this model was built in 1876. The most drastic change is in the roof style; these days one is more likely to see corrugated tin than the *jak*, nipa palm (*Nipa fruticans*)[114] fronds seen here. In general, rural Thai houses are raised off of the ground with pillars. The space beneath the house is used as a work area, storage area, and animal pen. The main floor usually has an open plan with broad expanses of teak flooring. The kitchen usually consists of a clay stove fueled by charcoal located either in an interior alcove or in a covered area on a wooden porch.

[114] Burkill 1966, Vol II, p. 1584.

APPENDIX:
KINGS OF THE CHAKRI DYNASTY

	Dates of reign:
Rama I, Buddha Yot Fa Chulalok Maharaj	r. 1782-1809
Rama II, Buddha Loet La Naphalai	r. 1809-1824
Rama III, Phra Nang Klao	r. 1824-1851
Rama IV, Mongkut	r. 1851-1868
Rama V, Chulalongkorn Maharaj	r. 1868-1910
Rama VI, Vajiravudh	r. 1910-1925
Rama VII, Prajadhipok	r. 1925-1935
Rama VIII, Ananda Mahidol	r. 1935-1946
Rama IX, Bhumibol Adulyadej	r. 1946-

REFERENCES CITED

Adovasio, J. M.
1977   **Basketry Technology: A Guide to Identification and Analysis.** Chicago: Aldine.

Allison, Effie B.
1977   "Chinese Ceramics Carried by the Dutch East India Company." **Arts of Asia,** 7, no. 6: 80-88.

Annez, Philippe
1994   **Some Splendid Crafts of the "SUPPORT" Foundation of Her Majesty Queen Sirikit of Thailand.** Bangkok: The Siam Society.

Atil, Esin, W. T. Chase, and Paul Jett
1985   **Islamic Metalwork in the Freer Gallery of Art.** Washington, D.C.: Smithsonian Institution.

Bekker, Sarah M.
1983   "Royal Gifts From Thailand" [Exhibition review of 1982 Smithsonian Exhibition]. **Oriental Art** 29, no. 2: 194-197.

Benedict, Burton
1983   **The Anthropology of World's Fairs.** Berkeley: University of California Press.

Bhongbhibat, Vimol, Bruce Reynolds, and Sukhon Polpatpicharn
1982   **The Eagle and the Elephant: 150 Years of Thai-American Relations.** Bangkok: United Production.

Bowring, Sir John
1857   **The Kingdom and Peoples of Siam.** London: 2 vols.

Brus, Rene
1985   "The Royal Regalia of Thailand." **Arts of Asia** 15, no. 5: 92-99.

Burhibad, Luang Boribal, and A. B. Griswold
1968   **The Royal Monasteries and Their Significance.** Thai Culture, new series, no. 2. Bangkok: The Fine Arts Department.

Burkill, I. H.
1966   **Dictionary of the Economic Products of the Malay Peninsula.** 2 vols. Kuala Lumpur: Ministry of Agriculture and Co-Operatives.

Cadet, J. M.
1970   **The Ramakien: The Thai Epic, Illustrated with the Bas-Reliefs of Wat Phra Jetubon, Bangkok.** Toyko: Kodansha

Carter, Cecil
1904   **The Kingdom of Siam.** Siamese Section, Ministry of Agriculture, Louisiana Purchase Exposition. New York: G.P. Putnam, Sons.

Chakrabongse, H. R. H. Prince Chula
1967   **Lords of Life: A History of the Kings of Thailand.** London: Alvin Redman.

Chandler, David P.
1982   "Cambodia's Relations with Siam in the Early Bangkok Period: The Politics of a Tributary State." **Journal of the Siam Society.** 60, no. 1:153-169.

Chanthawit, Natthaphat
1995   **Rua Phraratchaphithi (Royal Barges).** Bangkok Fine Arts Department.

Chomchai, Prachoom
1965   **Chulalongkorn the Great.** East Asian Cultural Studies Series, no. 8. Tokyo: The Center for East Asian Cultural Studies.

Cooler, Richard M.
1986   **The Use of Karen Drums in the Royal Courts and Buddhist Temples of Burma and Thailand: A Continuing Mon Tradition"** Michigan Papers on South and Southeast Asia no. 25. Ann Arbor: Center for South and Southeast Asian Studies, University of Michigan.
1995   **The Karen Bronze Drums of Burma: Types, Iconography, Manufacture and Use.** Leiden: E.J. Brill.

Cornell University Archives, Accession Records

Cosenza, Mario, ed.
1930   **The Complete Journal of Townsend Harris; First American Consul and Minister to Japan.** New York: The Japan Society and Charles E. Tuttle Company.

Crawfurd, John
1824   **Journal of an Embassy from the Governor-General of India to the Courts of Siam and Cochin China.** London.

Davis, Bonnie, et al
1995   **Royal Barges.** Bangkok: Foreign News Division, Government Public Relations Department, Office of the Prime Minister.

Delort, Robert
1992   **The Life and Lore of the Elephant.** New York: Harry N. Abrams.

Dhammadhibet, Prince
n.d. (1995) Verses for the Royal Barge Procession, trans. Khunying Chamnongsri Rutnin. Bangkok: Office of the Private Secretary to Her Majesty Queen Sirikit.

Dhaninivat Kromamun Bidyalabh Bridhyakorn, H.R.H. Prince
1948   "The Shadow Play as a Possible Origin to the Masked Play." **Journal of the Siam Society.** Volume 37, Part 1, pp. 26-32.

Dhaninivat Kromamun Bidyalabh Bridhyakorn, H. R. H. Prince, and Dhanit Yupho
1954   **The Khon.** Thailand Culture Series, # 11, Bangkok: The National Culture Institute.

Diskul, H. S. H. Prince Subhadradis, and Charles S. Rice
1982   **The Ramakian (Ramayana) Mural Paintings Along the Galleries of the Temple of the Emerald Buddha,** Revised Edition. Bangkok: Government Lottery Office, Kingdom of Thailand.

Fern, Alan
1991   "Presidential Gifts in America". In Thatcher and Taylor, pp. 48-49.

Fraser-Lu, Sylvia
1983   "Frog Drums and Their Importance in Karen Culture." **Arts of Asia**. 13 no. 5: 50-63
1988   **Handwoven Textiles of South-East Asia.** Singapore: Oxford University Press.
1989   **Silverware of Southeast Asia.** Singapore: Oxford University Press.

Fraser-Lu, Sylvia, and Sonia Krug
1982   "Thai Mother-of-Pearl". **Arts of Asia.** 12, no. 1, 73-81.

Gallop, Annabel
1994   **The Legacy of the Malay Letter.** London: The British Library and the National Archives of Malaysia.

Gerini, G.E.
1912   **Siam and Its Productions, Arts, and Manufactures: A Descriptive Catalogue of the Siamese Section at the International Exhibition of Industry and Labor Held in Turin April 29-November 1911.** Hertford: Stephen Austin & Sons.

Gittinger, Mattiebelle, and H. Leedom Lefferts, Jr.
1992   **Textiles and the Tai Experience in Southeast Asia.** Washington, D.C.: The Textile Museum.

Graca, Jorge
1977   "The Portuguese Porcelain Trade with China." **Arts of Asia.** 7, no. 6: 45-51.

Grehan, M. A.
1870   **Le Royaume de Siam.** Paris: Challamel Aine.

Griswold, Alexander B.
1960   **King Mongkut of Siam.** New York: The Asia Society.

Hall, Kenneth R.
1985   **Maritime Trade and State Development in Early Southeast Asia.** Honolulu: University of Hawaii Press.

Hall, Kenneth R., and John K. Whitmore, eds.
1976   **Explorations in Southeast Asian History: The Origins of Southeast Asian Statecraft.** Michigan Papers on South and Southeast Asia, No. 1. Ann Arbor: Center for South and Southeast Asian Studies, University of Michigan.

Hodges, Nan Powell, ed.
1991   **The Voyage of the Peacock: A Journal by Benjah Ticknor, Naval Surgeon.** Ann Arbor: University of Michigan Press.

Jessup, Helen Ibbsen
1990   **Court Arts of Indonesia.** New York: Harry N. Abrams.
1991   "Indonesian Court Arts." In Thatcher and Taylor, pp. 45-47.

Kalyanamitra, Joti
1977   **Six Hundred Years of Thai Artists.** Bangkok: The Fine Arts Commission of the Association of Thai Architects.

Krairiksh, Busaya, ed.
1985   **Kings of the Royal House of Chakri.** Nine vols. Bangkok: The SUPPORT Foundation.

Mauss, Marcel
1967   **The Gift.** New York: W. W. Norton & Co., Inc.

Maxwell, Robyn
1990   **Textiles of Southeast Asia: Tradition, Trade, and Transformation.** Canberra: Australian National Gallery, Melbourne: Oxford University Press.

McFarland, George Bradley, M.D.
1944   **Thai-English Dictionary.** Stanford, Calif.: Stanford University Press.

McQuail (Taylor), Lisa
1991   "Articles of Peculiar Excellence: The Siam Exhibit at the U. S. Centennial Exposition." **Journal of the Siam Society** 79, pt. 2: 13-23.
1995   **King Bhumibol Adulyadej Visits the United States of America: A Souvenir Album.** Washington, DC: The Office of Information, Royal Thai Embassy, for the Government Public Relations Department, Office of the Prime Minister.

Melikian-Chirvani, Assadullah Souren
1982   **Islamic Metalwork from the Iranian World: Eighth-Eighteenth Centuries.** London: Victoria and Albert Museum.

Moffat, Abbot Low
1961   **Mongkut, the King of Siam.** Ithaca, N. Y.: Cornell University Press.

Norton, Frank H. (ed.)
1876   **Frank Leslie's Illustrated Historical Register of the United States Centennial Exposition, 1876.** Reprinted 1974. New York: Paddington Press.

O'Kane, John
1972   **The Ship of Suleiman.** Persian Heritage Series, no. 11. New York: Columbia University Press.

Rabibhandana, Akin
1969   **The Organization of Thai Society in the Early Bangkok Period.** Data Paper No. 74. Ithaca, New York: Southeast Asian Program, Department of Asian Studies, Cornell University.

Reid, Anthony
1988   **Southeast Asia in the Age of Commerce, 1450-1680: Vol. I: The Lands Below the Winds.** New Haven: Yale University Press.
1993   **Southeast Asia in the Age of Commerce, 1450-1680: Vol. II: Expansion and Crisis.** New Haven: Yale University Press

Smith, George Vidal
1977   **The Dutch in Seventeenth-Century Thailand.** De Kalb: Northen Illinois University.

Smithies, Michael, and Euayporn Kerdchouay
1972   "Nang Talung: The Shadow Theatre of Southern Thailand." **Journal of the Siam Society** 60, Pt 1: 379-90.

Smithies, Michael
1990   **The Siamese Embassy to the Sun King: The Personal Memorials of Kosa Pan.** Bangkok: Editions Duang Kamol.

Smithsonian Institution Archives, Accession Records, National Museum of Natural History, Department of Anthropology Ethnology Collections, Siam collection.

Tambiah, S. J.
1976   **World Conquerer and World Renouncer: A Study of Budd-hism and Polity in Thailand Against a Historical Background.** New York: Cambridge University Press.

Tarling, Nicholas, ed.
1992   **The Cambridge History of Southeast Asia: Vol II: The Nine-teenth and Twentieth Centuries.** New York: Cambridge University Press.

Taylor, Paul Michael, and Lorraine V. Aragon
1991   **Beyond the Java Sea: Art of Indonesia's Outer Islands.** Washington, D.C.: National Museum of Natural History; New York: Harry N. Abrams.

Taylor, Paul Michael
1991   "Perspectives on the Gift in Indonesia and Beyond." In Thatcher and Taylor pp. 3-14.

Thatcher, Patricia, and Taylor, Paul Michael, eds.
1991   **The Gift as Material Culture.** Yale-Smithsonian Reports on Material Culture, no. 4. Washington, D.C. and New Haven, Connecticut: Yale-Smithsonian Seminar on Material Culture.

U.S. Library of Congress Archives, Accession Records.

U. S. National Archives, Ceremonial Letters: King Mongkut 1856.

U. S. National Archives, RG # 59, Consular Dispatches: Roberts, 1833; Chandler, 1857, 1859; Partridge 1861.

U. S. Navy
1876   **Exhibits of Articles Generally Used in Siam and of Samples of Trade of Siamese Origin Prepared by Order of His Majesty the King of Siam.** Philadelphia: J. B. Lippincott & Co.

Varnvaidya
1941   "The General System of Phonetic Transcription of Thai Characters into Roman." Bangkok: **The Journal of the Thailand Research Society,** 33(1). 49-65.

Viola, Herman J.
1984   **The National Archives of the United States.** New York: Harry N. Abrams.

Wales, H.G. Quaritch
1931   **Siamese State Ceremonies: Their History and Function.** London: Bernard Quaritch, Ltd.

Warren, William
1988   **The Grand Palace.** Bangkok: Office of His Majesty's Principal Private Secretary.

Wilson, Constance
1970   **State and Society in the Reign of Mongkut, 1851-1868: Thailand on the Eve of Modernization.** Ph.D. Dissertation, Modern History, Cornell University.

Winichakul, Thongchai
1994   **Siam Mapped: A History of the Geo-body of a Nation.** Honolulu: University of Hawaii Press; Chaing Mai: Silkworm Books.

Wood, William Maxwell, M.D., U.S.N.
1859   **Fankwei; or The San Jacinto in the High Seas of India, China, and Japan.** New York: Harper and Brothers.

Wray, Elizabeth, Clare Rosenfield, and Dorothy Bailey
1979   **Ten Lives of the Buddha.** Tokyo: Weatherhill.

Wright, Michael
1979   "Towards a History of Siamese Gilt-Lacquer Painting." **Journal of the Siam Society:** 67, pt 1:17-45.

Wyatt, David K.
1975   **The Crystal Sands: The Chronicles of Nagara Sri Dharmaraja** Data Paper no. 98. Ithaca, N.Y.: Southeast Asia Program, Department of Asian Studies, Cornell University.
1984   **Thailand: A Short History.** New Haven and London: Yale University Press.

Yukala et al.
1984   **Treasures of the Chakri Dynasty.** Bangkok, Royal Palace Press.

Yupho, Dhanit
1954   **The Preliminary Course in Training in Thai Theatrical Art:** Thailand Culture Series, no. 15. Bangkok: The National Culture Institute.
1968   **The Development of the National Museums in Thailand.** Thai Culture, new series, no. 24. Bangkok: Thai Fine Arts Department.
1989   **Khon Masks.** Bangkok: Thai Fine Arts Department.